OCCUPATIONAL DISEASES AND HEALTH AWARENESS THROUGH MULTIMEDIA

A Case Study among Women at Risk Employed in Coir Retting in Kerala, India

DR. DIVYA C. SENAN

PARTRIDGE
A Penguin Random House Company

To order additional copies of this book, contact
Partridge India
000 800 10062 62
www.partridgepublishing.com/india
orders.india@partridgepublishing.com

Contents

FOREWORD

The book **"Occupational Diseases and Health Awareness through Multimedia: A Case Study among Women at Risk Employed in Coir Retting in Kerala, India"** tries to bring home awareness of occupational diseases connected with coir industry through an innovative interactive multimedia application. Over the last quarter of a century technology involving application of multimedia has developed in leaps and bounds and particularly in the last decade its use has become so widespread reaching practically every citizen and covering every walk of life. A multimedia designer needs to rapidly explore numerous design ideas early in the design process, as creating an innovative design is the corner stone of creating an innovative multimedia learning platform itself. Dr. Divya C.Senan, Assistant Professor, Sree Narayana Training College has undertaken literally a challenge to give awareness to the coir workers, especially the women workers on the health hazards using a multimedia application. It has been proved in her study that the package is effective in making awareness among the target population.

A teacher being a social engineer is responsible to the whole society. Even though extension work is considered part of the responsibility of teachers in higher education, practically few teachers involve in such activities. Teachers are expected to involve in social awareness activities which benefit the students as well as community. The multimedia application prepared by Dr. Divya C.Senan as part of her UGC Minor Project intends to promote awareness on health and well-being among individuals, communities and populations, enabling them to address the broad determinants of health in order to reduce the vulnerability and risks to ill health and disability throughout the life cycle, especially among women. Usually such project reports slumber in some dust laden store houses. Here, she has undertaken a laudable initiative by authoring the present book which will enable its readers to have a close look at the coastal women engaged in coir industry and an innovative awareness programme. The coastal women are at risk population, so vulnerable to over work and exploitation from family and society. To combat the very common occupational diseases, they have to be made aware about it. Within the government and outside, use of multimedia application for alerting women at risk and explaining to them the common occupational diseases is very appreciable and it is really necessary to sensitize every person concerned about the different risk factors.

In this respect, the unique book prepared by Dr. Divya C.Senan is a timely and appropriate intervention. In very lucid style she has succeeded in explaining the basic concepts and theories related with multimedia applications very comprehensively. With excellent references and review of related studies this book could provide every reader to enlarge his knowledge to be prepared to understand and deal with normal threats and associated health risks.

The author has made all efforts to organize the book in a clear and easy to use format. The future and current professionals and other avid readers will be using it for understanding the interesting topic which would be rewarding them as well as reassuring the efforts made by the author by generating adequate serious interest in this important topic.

Dr.ASHA J.V
Asst. Professor & Hon.Director
Curriculum Development Centre
Dept. of Education, University of Kerala

PREFACE

Kerala is a major coconut producing state of India. Kerala coast is strikingly bordered by a string of backwaters, generally running parallel to the shoreline. The backwaters of Kerala provide water front for several major and small scale industries, amongst which coir retting industry ranks first. It is an important sector as far as economy of Kerala is concerned. Most of the coir workers are from socially and economically backward classes. The industry provides direct employment to more than 3.5 lakhs workers, majority of whom are female, who find this as the their principal source of income. The raw material for the industry is obtained by immersing the husk in water for 8-9 months. Here, mainly conventional methods of retting are practiced. Retting of husk presents unique and extremely serious problems along the coastal belt, changing the hydro ecology of the water body. Besides the ecological degradation caused by the liberation of organic wastes during the retting process, the unhygienic conditions prevailing around the area results in health hazard problems to the people engaged in this cottage industry. In the retting sites, aquatic pollution is caused due to organic wastes like lignin, tannin and polyphenols. Low pH and oxygen content, high BOD, chloride and alkalinity leads to anoxic condition, adversely affecting the flora and fauna. Air pollution also prevails in these areas due to the release of hydrogen sulphide, methane and carbon dioxide. Common diseases likely to occur among the people are filariasis, eye diseases, skin diseases, oedema of lungs and headache due to the inhalation of poisonous gases. It was found that the unhygienic conditions prevailing around the area results in health hazard problems to the people engaged in this cottage industry.

The most striking aspect of the retting industry is that the workers in the retting site spend almost the whole day in the yard and find hardly any time to spare for other educational and cultural activities. The wages given to them are very low compared to their hard work. As a natural consequence their living conditions are never improved. Their financial and epidemiological conditions remain to be very low. The area around the retting yards is inhabited mainly by the community engaged in coir industry. Hence, job related diseases are likely to occur among these people. Majority of the women are engaged in retting industry, irrespective of their age. Since they are spending almost the whole day in the unhygienic conditions prevailing in the yard they are at a high risk of developing occupational diseases. Their lack of knowledge about health and hygiene serves as the prime reason for the contagious diseases. From review of related studies it was revealed that the coir retting industry is an activity that is intricately interwoven with the social and economic structure. Field survey results indicated that 57 % of the sample suffered from job-oriented disease like skin disease, blindness, headache, back bone pains and respiratory disease. Rotted husk release more organic pollutants and they highly affect the water quality parameters. Therefore, it was a difficult task to save these women from these occupational hazards unless some new affordable technique is introduced. Majority of the households (70 %) fall within a low socio-economic status with a deepening poverty background depicted by low educational achievement and occupational status. Hence there arose the need to make them aware of the various health hazards, its causes and effects.

The search for a strategy which enables to give them awareness regarding health education results in an awareness program through multimedia. With the financial support of University Grants Commission, New Delhi, academic assistance of Sree Narayana Training College, Nedunganda and collaboration with local self-governance bodies, health centers and agencies like Coir fed, awareness campaigns were provided to the target group of coir retting industry with the help of the developed multimedia package on Health awareness of Occupational Diseases. This book is a report of the empirical study stated above. It gives a detail account of the design and development of the 'Health Literacy Package' and its implementation on the coir retting women. I hope the book is a ready reference for multimedia developers as well as for social activists who could use multimedia technology for social changes.

Dr.Divya C.Senan

Acknowledgment

*I bow my head before **Almighty** and my spiritual guide **Sree Narayana Guru** for all the blessings . . .*

The writing of this book, making its proposal, and preparing manuscripts were solitary activities. But before that during my research on this subject, I have received the help of many people.

*To start with, I greatly acknowledge **University Grants Commission, New Delhi** for the fund granted to carry out the research project. I extend my sincere thanks to **Sree Narayana Training College, Neduganda** for providing me the facilities needed for the work. I am very much grateful to the experts and personale related to medicine and coir industry especially, **Dr.K.Venugopal,** HOD & Medical Consultant, Department of Respiratory Medicine, Govt. General Hospital, Kochi, Ernakulam for extending his valuable opinion.*

*I would like to thank **Dr. Asha J.V**, Asst. Professor & Honorary Director, Curriculum Development Centre, Department of Education, University of Kerala, for her timely advice, insightful comments and support.*

*I am very thankful to **Girish Vijayan**, my husband for his invaluable help and never ending encouragement in the publication of the book. Love and thanks to my kids **Mihir &***

Milind who always adjusted with all my absence while I was hammering away at the computer.

*Finally, I am thankful to **Partridge India** for providing a vast and credible platform for this book to be published and read.*

Dr.Divya C.Senan

CHAPTER I

Introduction

The Small Scale Industries have been assigned an important role in India's development plans. Their development is one of the key strategies adopted by the Government, as they are a chief source of employment and income generation. The Coir Industry alone provides employment to about 5 lakhs of people especially women, and earns foreign exchange to the tune of Rs. 300 crores per annum. It is a highly labour intensive industry but the productivity levels in the industry are so low that the average earning of the workers, are insufficient to maintain even a subsistence standard of living. A rise in cost factors in the recent years has impacted the cost of production considerably, without any corresponding increase in productivity.

On the demand side, Coir Products appear to be facing tremendous global competition from other hard fibres. Also, price fluctuations seem to have become a perennial feature of the coir-markets. Marketing therefore has become a major problem in recent years and the future prospects of the industry depend on the expansion of domestic as well as the foreign markets. However, the industry in the developing economies is characterized by insufficient marketing, which has added to its already mounting problems. Firstly, the manufacturers of the original and the major product sector of the coir-household have a very low direct access to the markets. The Traders and Exporters control the entire marketing business due to their higher financial strength and procure goods only on job-work basis. The actual producers find it beyond their own means to hold the products for a long time before marketing it directly. Due to a limited access to market, the traditional yarn and other product manufacturers are always engaged in price-wars and are even found to compromise on quality aspects in order to make their products cheaper.

Secondly, the anti-pollution awareness has increased and the enforcements from the Government are a threat to the industry, especially due to the polluting nature of the Retting process. Another major concern is the amount of drudgery involved in the processes of retting and Fibre Extraction. Due to the insufficient technological upgradation, the manufacturers are unable to make these processes less labour intensive and environment friendly. As the interests of each sector in the Coir industry are different, therefore it does not seem feasible to organize them under the same umbrella. The smaller women groups with active intermediaries will have to be identified in order to initiate small yet productive activities. The untapped raw material potential in this cluster can be productively utilized with an active intervention from these groups. The two major NGOs in this cluster with wide network can contribute quite a lot in this respect.

Coir Industry in India has a very long history. Even the 11th Century A.D. Arab writers have mentioned about Coir and referred to the use of this material for ship's cables, fenders, rigging etc. During the Thirteenth century, there was an evidence of coir yarn being used for ship-building in the Persian Gulf. The remarkable international correspondent of ancient times, Marco Polo, was impressed by its usage there and later on visited the land where Arabs bought their coir and recorded as to how it was made out of a fibre extracted from the coconut husk. In fact till the early decades of the last century the industrial development in Kerala was mostly centered on coconuts. Production of coir yarn and fibre quietly spread through the coastal belt of Travancore utilizing the abundant and cheap labour that was available. Coir weaving industry was localized in and around Alleppey. Coir industry is one of the traditional industries of Kerala. This industry is described to be traditional, not merely in reference to its historical traditions but also in reference to their traditional technology base that continues to be handcrafted.

Availability of plenty of coconuts from the low land and hinter land, accessibility to good roads, numerous canals and rivers, the presence of brackish lakes and lagoons replenished by fresh water schemes and above all the presence of labour force with large experience in this industry have contributed greatly to the location of the Coir Industry in the coastal areas of the State." *(Patel S J, Report of the "Coconut and coconut products in India" GOI publication)*.Coir industry is concentrated mainly in the coastal belt of Kerala, Tamil Nadu, Andhra Pradesh and Orissa. The 10 coastal districts account for nearly 90 per cent of the total production in the State of Kerala. Kollam district supplies 8.06 per cent of the State production of coconuts while the Alleppey district, which has top most concentration of coir industry supplies only 6.5 per cent of the total production of coconuts in the State. The production of coconuts in the three regions viz. low land (covering coastal belt), midland and highland was about 54, 38 and 8 percent respectively *(Source: Department of Economic and Statistics, Government of Kerala)*. The Kollam district area covers the above three regions. The huge importance of the Coir industry in the economic development of Kerala is evident from the fact that it is a means of livelihood for a large section of its population and forms the basis of several other Small Scale and Cottage Industries. About two third of the Coir dependent households in the state belong to the Hindu backward section and only about 7 per cent to the Hindu forward.

Kerala has the highest density of population than any other state of India. Area of Kollam district alone forms 6.41 per cent of the total area of Kerala and accommodates 8.27 per cent of the total population of the state. The whole district looks like a continuous village of independent and separate households with frequent small towns. This makes the issue of Environmental Pollution of water, air and even noise, a really critical one for the area. Apart from the health aspect, it is important to keep the natural environment clean and beautiful in order to attract tourists also. The land, its fertility with evergreen vegetations and the clean waters of its rivers and lagoons are some of the most precious assets of Kollam and we should take full precautions to keep this beautiful balance of nature alive.

The Golden-fibre 'Coir' is all capable of becoming a medium for the attainment of the Millennium Goals of Cleaner and Greener Earth, Empowerment of Women and Bringing to the fore the weak and less privileged. Coir is a natural fibre and its application in whatever form or use makes the product naturally biodegradable.

Context of the Study

Kerala coast is strikingly bordered by a string of backwaters, generally running parallel to the shoreline. These water bodies locally known as Kayals occupy extensive areas. The size of these water bodies is significantly varied. Out of the 29 backwaters of the Kerala coast, seven are characteristically river mouth estuaries. The backwaters of Kerala provide water front for several major and small scale industries, amongst which coir retting industry ranks first. This industry provides employment to a large number of people, especially women folk. The raw material for the industry is obtained by immersing the husk in water for 8-9 months. Here, mainly conventional methods of retting are practiced. Retting of husk presents unique and extremely serious problems along the coastal belt, changing the hydro ecology of the water body. Besides the ecological degradation caused by the liberation of organic wastes during the retting process, the unhygienic conditions prevailing around the area results in health hazard problems to the people engaged in this cottage industry. A vast number of rural populations of coastal Kerala are engaged in retting industry, irrespective of their age. They find this work as the source of their principle income. Male members are associated with coolie work connected with coir industry, agriculture and fishing. The most striking aspect of the retting industry is that the workers in the retting site spent almost the whole day in the unhygienic conditions prevailing in the yard and find hardly any time to spare for other educational and cultural activities. The wages given to them are very low compared to their hard work. As a natural consequence their living conditions are never improved. Their financial and epidemiological conditions remain to be very low. The area around the retting yards is inhabited mainly by the community engaged in coir industry. Hence, job related diseases are likely to occur among these people. In the retting sites, aquatic pollution is caused due to organic wastes like lignin, tannin and polyphenols. Low pH and oxygen content, high BOD, chloride and alkalinity leads to anoxic conditions adversely affecting the flora and fauna. Air pollution also prevails in these areas due to the release of hydrogen sulphide, methane and carbon dioxide. Common diseases likely to occur among the people are filariasis, eye diseases, skin diseases, oedema of lungs and headache due to the inhalation of poisonous gases.

The Sree Narayana Training College, Nedunganda started in the name of His Holiness Sree Narayana Guru is situated in Anjengo panchayath which is a coastal region in Trivandrum district. As a part of the curricular studies the student teachers of our college went for a survey in Anjengo panchayath collecting data regarding the health condition as well as socio economic conditions of the inhabitants. It was found that the unhygienic conditions prevailing around the area results in health hazard problems to the people engaged in this cottage industry. Majority of the women are engaged in retting industry, irrespective of their age. Since they are spending almost the whole day in the unhygienic conditions prevailing in the yard they are at a high risk of developing occupational diseases. Their lack of knowledge about health and hygiene serves as the prime reason for the contagious diseases. From review of related studies it was revealed that the coir retting industry is an activity that is intricately interwoven with the social and economic structure. Field survey results indicated that 57 % of the sample suffered from job-oriented disease like skin disease, blindness, headache, back bone pains and respiratory disease. Rotted husk release more organic pollutants and they highly affect the water quality parameters. Therefore, it is a difficult task to save these women from these occupational hazards unless some new affordable technique is introduced. Majority of the households (70 %) fall within a low socio-economic status with a deepening poverty background depicted by low educational achievement and occupational status. Hence there arise the need to make them aware of the various health hazards, its causes and effects. The search for a strategy which enables to give them awareness regarding health education results in an awareness program through multimedia. This project aims in developing a multimedia package for health and hygiene for coastal women and to conduct awareness program with the help of the developed package on the target group of coir retting industry so as to empower them. The coming chapters give you a detailed report on the Coir industry in Kerala, design and development of a multimedia health awareness package and the awareness programme conducted among the women coir workers of Anjengo panchayat regarding occupational diseases.

Chapter II

Coir Industry in Kerala

2.1 INTRODUCTION

India stands second with respect to production of coconut among the coconut producing countries of the world(APCC statistical year book 1999).The crop provides livelihood to around 10 million people of the country who are engaged to cultivation, processing, marketing and other related activities. It contributes around Rs. 700 crores to the country's GDP. The crop earns valuable foreign exchange to the tune of about Rs. 313 crores by way of export, mainly coir and coir products". Small and marginal farmers dominate the coconut cultivation in India. It is estimated that there are around 35 to 45 lakhs of coconut farmers in Kerala alone.' The average holdings of more than 90 per cent of the coconut farmers are within five acres. They are unorganized, isolated and lack collective bargaining. In fact there are no organised wholesale markets for raw coconut in the country. The end products such as copra and coconut oil determine the price of coconut. There is no say for the coconut farmers in determining the price of their primary produce, viz., and coconut. It is the middlemen who determine the price of raw coconuts. In most cases, the farmers are bonded with the middlemen who have got standing arrangements with the farmers for the harvesting and disposal of the nuts. Coconut is grown in most of the states and Union Territories in India. However, the major share of coconut production is contributed by the four southern states Viz., Kerala, Karnataka, Tamil Nadu and Andhra Pradesh.

2.2 COIR INDUSTRY'S TRADITION

Coir, the golden fibre, extracted from coconut is classified as the industrial ropes, cordage for safe haulage and anchorage, manufacture of mats, carpets geo-textiles etc. Coir industry is the largest industry in the coast. Kerala with her favourable ecological setting, abundant supply of coconut, and cheap labour, has provided the necessary conditions for the growth development of the world's largest coir industry. The extraction of fibre from husk has a very long tradition here. Coir industry begins with dehusking, which is largely concentrated in Kerala as this state produces 6672 millions nuts of coconuts [45%] out of a total all-India production of 14924.8 million nuts". In addition to this, the facilities like lakes and lagoons for retting the husk and the availability of traditional expertise of the people in coir work also added to the growth of coir industry in Kerala. History tells that ancient Greece, Egypt and Rome used coir ropes made in Kerala for the construction of houses, citadels, ship mast and mansions. It was with the arrival of the Portguese in Kerala that the coir trade spread to the European countries. The British interest on Kerala's coir products made them conduct an exhibition on coir products in London in 1851. The Coir Industry of the country comprised of fibre making, yarn making, mats and mattings, rubber backed mats, synthetic backed mats rubberised bed sand various other products. The first coir factory in the country was started in1854 by an Irish man named James Darragh, at Kulachal, Alappuzha in Kerala.

In 1859 Darragh shifted his works to central Alappuzha, where along with his brother—in—law, Smail, organised a large coir factory for the manufacture of mats and mattings named James Darragh, Smail & Co. Ltd. with its offices in London and New York. The success of Darragh's company attracted many enterprising businessmen to Kerala to set up factories in the State for production and export of coir products. In course of time demand for coir and coir products increased and several coir factories in and around Alappuzha expanded and the number of units increased to 12607. It could also claim a lion's share in the total export from India during the period. During the post war period labour unions started putting forward several demands on behalf of labour and consequently factory owners felt that operation of large establishments would be uneconomic. This led to a process of retrenchment. In the course of a few years after independence the foreigners left the coir scene and most of the large factories were closed down or some of them were taken over by the worker's unions themselves and re-organized them on cooperative basis. But lack of competence of workers to manage the units on commercial basis had further affected the growth of coir sector in the country.

Coir exports were dwindling, the industry was languishing, large number of workers had lost their employment and crisis continued to deepen in the industry which led to prolonged agitations by the coir workers

2.3 VARIOUS STAGES OF COIR PRODUCTION

From the organizational point of view, the coir industry could broadly be divided into four sectors. The first sector is connected with retting of husks and production of fibre. The second sector is the hand spinning sector which comprises of about 80000 hand spinning households. Spindle Spinning of coir yam forms the third sector. The total number of workers in beating of retted husk and spinning of coir yarn is estimated to be around two third of the total workers in the coir industry. The fourth sector is concerned with the manufacture of coir mats and mattings. Majority of workers employed in the fibre extraction and spinning sector are women. Child labour also appears in these sectors.'

Spinning is cottage industry spread over a wide area along the backwaters of Kerala. But manufacturing is an organised industry concentrated in certain localities mainly Alappuzha Project area. The location of these sectors of industry seems purely in accordance with the Weberian theory." The basic raw material of coir industry is the coconut husk which has low value. There are various processes involved from collection of raw husk to manufacturing of yarn. The fibrous raw husk is extracted from nuts through the process called 'dehusking', a manual work. The coir fibre is five to ten inches in length. There are two major types of coir fibres. They are White and Brown fibre.

White Fibre

White Fibre is extracted from retted husk. Retting may be natural or chemical. In natural retting the husks are soaked in, preferably saline water for a certain period [average 8 to 10 months] until the fibre becomes loose and soft. Soaking of husks may be in three ways. One is immersing the husks in the muddy pits dug near lagoons in shallow water or by the side of backwaters where water flows in and out, with the rise and fall of the tide. An average pit contains about

1000 husks. The second method of soaking is, collecting the husks in coir net sand immersing them in water. The unit adopted for soaking in coir nets is usually10000 husks at a time. The other way of soaking which is practiced in some areas is, putting the husks in enclosures erected in shallow backwaters with coconut leaves and petioles. This method is known as "Valachukettu mude". After the husks are filled in the soaking pits, nets or enclosures, they are covered with coconut leaves and mud and weighed down to prevent floatation when immersed in water.

During the retting process, the husks become soft and a number of substances like carbohydrates, glucosides, tanins and nitrogen compounds are brought in solution. The time required for retting is influenced by various factors such as the stage of maturity of coconuts, the weather and the nature of water. Husks from immature nuts ret in short period. The process is quicker during the summer season because heat is necessary for fermentation. But the retting period is longer if the retting is done in saline water and shorter in fresh water. However, retting in saline water is considered to be the best for natural retting. The salts in the saline water prevent over-fermentation without discoloring the fibre and the resultant fibre is strong and better coloured as the pith and other impurities are continuously removed by the free flow of water due to tidal action. The retting site is not complete in fresh water and the fibre retains a certain amount of pith. For ensuring the quality of fibre, soaking is usually done in shallow waters as the heating effects of the sun on the water help to produce a better fibre. In shallow backwaters, it may sometimes happen that the husks soaked in pits get exposed during the low tide, which results in production of inferior quality fibre. This problem can be avoided if soaking is done in coir nets which helps to deep sink husks in backwaters and thereby subject to better tidal action than they are placed in pits. It was noticed that soaking crushed husks, reduces the retting period by six months. The crushing can be done by simple crushing rollers, similar to sugar cane crushers. White fibre is generally the longest and the fine stand they are suitable for spinning yam and products of superior quality.

Mechanical and chemical retting are adopted in areas where facilities for natural retting do not exist and for speedy retting. In mechanical method either dry husks or green husk are soaked in cement Tanks having a provision for water flow in and out from tank for a period of one to three weeks. This ensures a better circulation of water, which will come into contact with all the husks and remove the acids and gums deposited in them. It will be necessary to re-arrange the husks from the lower part of the tank to the upper part and vice versa from time to time. Medium to major coir units, practice this method. In some units, the husks are first crushed through iron rollers, a machine called husk crusher. Then the husks are thrown into a retting tank where they undergo fermentation for a minimum period of 72 hours. The fibre is extracted manually or mechanically. However, these processes do not yield fibre of spinnable quality as in the case of natural retting, but yield only bristle and mattress fibres."

In Chemical Retting, various methods are developed. The advantages claimed are of higher yield of, uniform quality fibre and considerable saving of time. But the financial advantages of chemical retting compared to the natural process has not been fully investigated for commercial exploitation. In one method the green or dry husks are partially crushed and treated under steam pressure of 5.6 to 7.0 Kg/cm with sodium sulphate or sodium carbonate containing a trace of aluminium sulphate for one to two hours. During this process, the pith is loosened from the fibre and removed by washing. The fibre obtained is of good quality but bit darker than that of natural retting.

Another method of chemical retting is by means of technology developed by the Coir Board for reducing the retting period using a bacterial cocktail 'Coirret'. It is claimed that, it helps besides in the period of retting and assists to improve the quality of unretted brown fibre." Under this method the bundles of brown fibre produced from combing mills from Tamil Nadu or elsewhere are put into water in Cement Tank and allowed to be there for 72 hours with chemical

Coir rets. After the water is drained out the resultant fibre is claimed to have almost the same quality of natural fibre.

Extraction of White Fibre

Extraction of White Fibre involves the following processes:-

1. **Taking out of retted husk**

   After natural retting, the husks are taken out of water and washed to get rid of mud and dirt.

2. **Peeling**

   After natural retting the outer skin is then peeled off before beating.

3. **Husk Beating**

   After peeling, the husks are placed on wooden blocks and beaten with awooden mallet or iron rods till the fibres are separated from rotten pith and are then manually sifted. It is unhygienic hard work, usually done by women. One-person can beat 100 husk per day. While beating, the whole body will be covered with pith and smells foul. If the decomposed husks are not exposed to the sun for long, the extraction becomes difficult and the colour of the fibre darkens. The fibre so extracted is cleaned and then spread in shade for drying and occasionally beaten and tolled up with poles to remove the remnants of pit hand impurities still attached to the fibre.

4. **Willowing**

   For making superior type of fibre, especially for spinning, the fibre so obtained is combed in a specially designed combing or willowing machine. The willowing machine consists of a number of knives with saw-like teeth mounted on a wooden shaft set spirally and it is rotated by hand or motor.

5. **Machanised Husk Beating**

The fibre from the retted husk is also extracted mechanically with husk beating machine. The retted husk is passed between rollers and then the crushed husks are torn on rolling cylinders with nails on the cylinder casting. The raw coir fibre, thus obtained, is further cleaned by means of blowing fans. The machine helps to soften and remove the last traces of pith on the fibre and the processed fibres are clean. With a husk beating machine 10000 retted husk can be beaten up per day with 15 HP. Motor.

Brown Fibre
Extraction of Brown Fibre

Brown Fibre is extracted from ripe dry husk or partially retted husk by the mechanical defibering. These husks are fed into revolving drums provided with upright spikes of high carbon steel which tear out the outer skin and some of the pith, leaving the long coarse fibres. The accumulated mixed fibres that get piled up by the side of the machine are further processed in the willowing machine and separated into different grades. Brown fibre is extracted from ripe dry husk by the mechanical defibreing. It is having a brown colour and is of poor quality. It may be of two types—'Bristle' and 'Curled'. The bristle fibre is thick and long and is used for brush making. The 'Curled' fibre is shorter staple and finds use in the upholstery, mattresses etc.

2.3.1 Yield of Fibre from Husk

The yeild of fibre is subjected to considerable variation depending upon the season, method of extraction and quality of fibre produced. The yield from retted husk is more than that from unretted husks. The husk of coconut produced between the months of January to April is capable of getting top range) field. Taking all these variations into consideration, the average yield of white frbre from 1000 full husks in India is estimated at 81.8 kg. But Govt. of India [1999-2000] revealed that in Kerala the fibre—husk ratio is 86.72 kg. from 1000 husk, but it is 110 kg, 65.13 kg, 122 kg in Tamil Nadu, Andhra and Karnataka respectively.

2.3.2 Spinning of Coir Yarn

The spinning of coir yarn is a traditional cottage industry in India and is mostly concentrated in the backwater areas where natural retting is available.

Spinning processes are of three types:

(a) Hand Spinning, (b) Ratt Spinning [Wheel Spinning] and (c) Machine Spinning.

(a) Hand spinning

In hand spinning, fibre is rolled between the palms with a clockwise twist into strands of short length, when sufficient quantity is made for the work of a day, the strands are taken in pairs and twisted together in the opposite direction to form a 2—ply yarn. The yarn is then held in position by the toes and individual pieces of yarn are joined together one after another by continuing the counter twist using both palms till the required length for knot or mud [6 to 18meters] is reached. The yam is then reeled in the form of a hank and a knot is made at the end. One worker is estimated to produce about 2 to 2.5 kg. of yarn per day. Hand spun yarn is soft and has uniformity of twist and thickness. This is considered as the top quality yam. Since it is not remunerative the workers are not ready for doing this work. More over the coir workers skilled in hand spinning are also rare.

(b) Ratt (Wheel) Spinning

In ratt spinning two ratts are used—one ratt with two spindles are fitted to a stationary stand and the other one with one spindle is mounted on wheels and can be moved forward and backward. In the actual working, one boy or girl rotates the wheel on the stationary stand by rotating a handle fixed to its axis. Two adults make the strands by hooking short length of fibre strands on to the spindles of the stationery ratt and walking back, delivers the fibre continuously to form strands of uniform thickness. During this process, the stationary ratt is made to rotate continuously to give the necessary twist to the strand. When the two adults complete a length of about 15—16m of the strand each, the rotation of the stationery wheel is stopped. The two ends of the single strands are then joined together and hooked to the spindle of the movable ratt. One adult worker takes charge of this movable ratt and it is now slowly rotated to give the two strands yam a twist in a direction to that of the single strands. The other worker in charge of the yam who moves forward towards the stationary wheel with yarn guide in hand held between the two strands yarn. The yarn guide is a triangular block of wood, grooved on the sides known as 'Achue'. It helps to regulate the counter twist, prevents knots and kinks and binds the strands very close. The worker keeps a steady movement of the yarn guide towards the stationary ratt, followed by the forward movement of the movable ratt to allow the contraction of the yam in the process of doubling operation. These movements are simultaneously carried out by rotation of the stationary ratt also, in order to prevent the loosening of the twist on the single strands while imparting the doubling twist by the operation of the movable wheel. These movements are controlled by experienced workers. The spun yam lengths of 12 to 15 m. is reeled intohanks. About100strands of 15 m. each weighting about 15 kg can be produced per day. This is the popular method of yam spinning. However, it does not possess the evenness and softness of the former type of yarn. The inherent defect of this method is that it requires a long open yard, the length of which limits the maximum length of the strands, which may come around 15 meters. Therefore the process of production is also interrupted during monsoon to those who are not having such a lengthy shed. The grading of coir yam, is made according to colour, rummage,· moisture content and the presence of sand, salt etc. A large number of yarn types are available in India and are recognized according to its place of manufacture.

(c) **Mechanized Spinning (Motorized Ratt)**

Mechanised Spinning is developed by Coir Board in order to avoid unnecessary movement of coir workers, to save moving space of yard, to increase productivity and to save the cost of production. In this method of spinning 0.5 H.P. motor is used to rotate the spindle carrying fibre strands. A basket is attached to the machine to carry the fibre. The woman worker sitting alongside the machine issues fibre to the spindle and the yam is produced by operating 'on 'and 'off 'position of the switch by the leg. The yarn produced by motorized ratt is rough and thick and is not attractive to users and productivity is lower than traditional method. This is because from 30 Kg. of Fibre the yarn product will be only 20 to 22Kg. whereas from traditional spinning yarn the product will be 26 to 28 kg.

2.3.3 Drying and Bundling of Yarn

Drying of yarn in the sunshine is inevitable for maintenance of quality of the fibre. After proper drying the yarn is bundled weighing usually 15 Kg. or 30Kg. per bundle

2.4 EMPLOYMENT IN THE COIR INDUSTRIAL SECTOR

Coir Industry is the largest cottage industry in the country. It is concentrated in the coconut producing states and provides employment to about5:2900persons. Of this, Kerala accounts for 76 per cent, Tamil Nadu, 12 per cent 23and all other states accounts 12 per cent. Eighty five per cent of the coir workers in Kerala are women (3, 25,000). The socio-economic conditions of coir workers are generally found to be very poor and most of them live below poverty line. They use the first chance to migrate from this sector to other sectors.

2.5 SOCIO-ECONOMIC CONDITIONS OF COIR WORKERS

In Kerala nearly two lakh households' are depending upon coir as their livelihood. Ninety per cent of the workers in the coir industry are engaged in the retting of husks, extraction of fibre and spinning of yarn etc. and majority of them are women. There are 23000 retting units, existing in about 357 villages' spread over the coastal area of the State." The notable feature of these villages is the absence of an alternate employment opportunity when there is no possibility of coir related work and so living in poverty. Majorities of the coir workers are members of Coir Vyavasaya Societies. These societies are encouraged by Government by providing various types of financial assistance for giving full—time employment and fair wages to them. Even then the coir workers are living in poor socio-economic circumstances.

2.6 SEASONAL NATURE OF EMPLOYMENT

A majority of the Coir-workers engaged in spinning work in household units itself. The spinning activities are conducted in open yards and prolonged adverse weather conditions affect the production. During monsoons, the extraction of fibre and spinning of yarn in the open yard is possible only for temporary durations. The employment rate of the Coir Spinners is directly linked to the rate of demand in the product sector. Especially in the case of products that are manufactured against specific export orders, there is a high rate of fluctuation observed and workers do not get assured employment throughout the year. The creation of regular employment can be made possible through the following measures:

- Modernisation of technology in Spinning and Product sector.
- Finding new user areas for Coir such as Coir-geo-textile, Pith composting, Polymer Composite Board etc.
- Capturing the untapped export as well as domestic potential in the markets.

2.7 MANAGING PROCESSING WASTES

Coir Pith is a waste material and huge accumulation of the pith causes environmental problems. The extraction of 1 Kg of Coir fibre generates more than 2 Kg of Coir Pith. Since Coir Pith contains about 25% Lignin, it does not decompose easily. With a view to finding solution for the problematic waste material, Central Coir Research Institute (CCRI) has developed a technology to convert the Coir Pith into organic manure within 30 days, by applying a fungus known as "Pith-plus". This is being produced on commercial basis at the pilot scale laboratory at CCRI. Popularization of this innovation is being done by the Extension Task Force of CCRI. This should be strengthened in Kollam cluster where retting and fibre extraction is being done at the coastal areas.

2.8 ENVIRONMENTAL HAZARDS RELATED TO COIR INDUSTRY

In recent years public attention has been focused increasingly on environmental pollution and its impact on human beings, animals and plant kingdom. The environment can be defined as "the aggregate of all external conditions and influences, affecting the life and development of an organism, human behavior or society".20The major environmental pollution is related to coir industry is contamination of water and air through husk retting. While immersing coconut husk in the lagoons and backwater side for months and years, the water will be highly contaminated. When surface water is polluted, consequently it leads contamination of ground water. Ground water pollution as an impairment of water quality by chemicals, heat or bacteria to a degree, that does not necessarily create an actual public health hazard, but does adversely affect such waters for domestic, farm, municipal or industrial use. Pollution can originate from a point or distributed sources within the recharge area. The ground water moves very slowly, sometimes many years may lapse after the start of pollution before affected water shows up in a well. Similarly, many years may be required to rehabilitate contaminated aquifers, after the sources of pollution have been eliminated. Coir industry has a history of one and half century in Kerala. Uninterrupted retting activity in the lagoons led to contamination of surface water. While visiting these places in Kollam, Chirayinkeezhu, Karunagapally, A1appuzha, Vaikom,

Kozhikode etc. one will feel foul smell, see black water in the place of very transparent water. We can walk through these places only with closed nose. In these places it is learnt that one can't depend water from well, which is also likely affected due to pollution. After some more years the households may force abandonment of wells and may require costly development of alternate water supplies. This polluted atmosphere in air and water which hinder tourism development in the State, as lagoons and backwaters are the real attraction to the tourists. In some of the areas of coir industry like Thanneermukkom environmentalists started protest against carrying out retting activity in lagoons and backwaters.

2.9 HEALTH HAZARDS

Coir industry is a predominant industry in many parts of southern Kerala. It has been noticed earlier that there is increased incidence of nasobronchial allergy among the population involved in this industry. Huge amount of dust is generated during various stages of coir manufacture. Various chemicals are also used. This is in contrast to the only published study among coir workers conducted by Uragoda CG, involving 779 workers who processed coir in Colombo; which states that coir dust was inert and therefore not harmful to man. But most of the studies indicate that coir dust can evoke allergic symptoms and pulmonary function abnormalities. Pulmonary function defect in the majority of coir workers included a reversible airway obstruction with predominant small airway obstruction. Allergic reaction to one of the organic components of the coir dust is a factor. The presence of allergic nasal symptoms and the sequential emergence of asthmatic symptoms later support this theory of allergic origin. Allergic or hypersensitivity reaction to a possible fungal element in the moist dusty atmosphere is yet another cause. Non-allergic bronchial hyper-reactivity following exposure to chemicals and particulate dust. Sulphur dioxide which is being used in this industry for bleaching of coir fibres might have implications on pulmonary functions. Poor working condition also may contribute to the symptoms.

Combined nasal and bronchial symptoms are noticed among majority of symptomatic coir workers. Functional abnormality is predominantly obstruction with significant reversibility. Reduction in pulmonary function is directly proportional to the duration of work. Exposure to chemicals hastens the disease process and increases the severity of disease. The nasobronchial symptoms in coir industry may be considered as an occupational hazard. Even though, in absence of bronchial challenge testing, it may be inappropriate to label coir work as occupational hazard.

Asthma is well known to occur as a result of exposure to certain vegetable dusts of occupational origin. Therefore a close inquiry was made from the workers as to any history suggestive of this condition. There were six men with asthma, two of whom had it prior to their employment in the industry and therefore it could not be related to exposure to coir dust. Further, their attacks eased off in spite of regular exposure to the dust. Another two cases gave a family history of asthma. Their attacks occurred at fairly wide intervals though they worked regularly at the factory. Therefore it is unlikely that their attacks were precipitated by coir dust. In the remaining two cases there was no definite indication whether the asthma was related to coir dust or not. Asthma is a fairly common condition in Sri Lanka, and an incidence of six cases (0-8 %) among 779coir workers is consistent with the incidence in the general population. Chronic bronchitis. Chronic bronchitis is seldom diagnosed in Sri Lanka, mainly because of low consumption of smoking tobacco and relative freedom from atmospheric pollution. There were only three cases of chronic bronchitis in the coir workers examined.

Byssinosis is caused by dusts from vegetable fibres such as cotton, flax, and soft hemp, workers were closely questioned regarding symptoms suggestive of this condition. The factories operated three eight-hour shifts, and they were closed on Saturday afternoons and Sundays but none of the workers gave a history of Monday fever. The medical officer had not come across a single case of byssinosis, and the manager and supervisors were unaware of any such symptoms in the workers. Thus there is no clinical evidence to suggest the presence of byssinosis among coir workers. In this respect coir appears to belong to the same group as sisal, jute, and hard hemp.

In a study about pulmonary tuberculosis among coir workers, there were nine cases with definite evidence of pastor present tuberculosis among the 779 coir workers. All of them had contracted the disease during their period of employment as coir workers. This prevalence is similar to that in the general population in Sri Lanka. Eight of the nine affected workers belonged to the small factory where 281 workers were examined, while there was only one case among the498 workers in the large factory. If exposure to coir dust carried an increased risk of tuberculosis, then one would have expected a more even distribution of cases in the two factories where the average period of service of each set of workers was similar, namely10-1 and 11-8 years respectively.

The coir workers do not use masks mainly due to lack of awareness. Besides, handling of dye chemicals used for colouring of coir yarn and coir products also lead to asthmatic and allergic diseases.

CHAPTER III

Coir Industry and Related Studies

3.1 INTRODUCTION

The review of literature involves the systematic identification, location and analysis of documents which include periodicals, abstracts, reviews, books and other research reports. The major purpose of reviewing the literature is to determine what has already been done that relates to the thrust area of a study. It not only avoids unintentional duplication, but it also provides the understandings and insights necessary for the logical framework into which the problem fits. It also points out research strategies and specific procedures and measuring instruments that have and have not been found to be productive in investigating the problem (Gay, 1996). Being familiar with previous research also facilitates the interpretation of results.

A brief account of the relevant literature reviewed is presented below

3.2 STUDIES RELATED TO COIR INDUSTRY

Unnithan (1970) in his book examines the various factors related to coir industry in the country. Background of the setting up of coir industry like locational factors, the various processes in the manufacture of coir and coir products, marketing structure and organisation of the industry etc. are covered in his work. It presents an analytical study of the cost of production of different varieties of coir and coir products. According to him coir industry is not an organised industry in the modem sense of the term and functions under the setup of an under-developed country. Coir production is multi-staged and extends from the production of coconuts to the making of coir yam for the manufacture of mats. The study is mainly of a general nature and does not analyse any aspects mentioned above in detail. As a result it does not suggest any policy measures for better prospects.

Pylee (1975), in his work examined the various aspects of the coir industry, viz., the structure, export, internal consumption of coir goods, marketing channel, labour force and crisis of the coir industry. The study stressed the necessity for strengthening the base for export production by manufacturing sophisticated coir products through modernization. The report also stressed the need for making Kerala products cheaper than European coir products and developing a stable domestic market for coir products in India. The Report listed various government orders and notifications relating to coir industry in India. The study also emphasised the need for undertaking Research and Development in coir sector.

Thampan (1984) also gives a detailed description of different varieties of coir fibre, scientific process of retting [Mechanical and Chemical Methods], process of extraction of fibre [White Fibre and Brown Fibre], use of piths etc. in his book. The book generated awareness of the varieties of fibre and grades, chemical composition, methods of spinning coir yam (through traditional hand spinning and ratt spinning) and their advantages. It also gives an insight into the varied uses of coconut palm to the people.

Thampan (1988) in another work offers a detailed account of production of coconut in various countries and states in India. He reveals that from estimation, about 10 million people depend directly or indirectly on coconut cultivation and industry for their livelihood and this crop has profound influence on the agricultural economy of many states. His study also gives the rate of yield per hector in various parts of India, number of retting yards, and copra processing units in Kerala.

Thomas Issac *et al* (1992), in their book "Modernisation and Employment" explain the crisis in Kerala's coir industry. This book draws the features of the industry during the fifties, traditional process of coir production, the relevance of coir industry in the economy of Kerala, the pitiable conditions of coir workers and improvement in the conditions of the workers through the leadership of militant trade unionism. It reviews the socio—political, economic and technological factors that affect trends in the coir industry in Kerala. To impart relevance of the industry it cites the value of shipments of coir from Malabar Coast from 1889-1950. It mentions the untapped husk potential in Kerala and suggests that through appropriate measures, the industrial utilization of husk can be increased. This book expresses the view that the policy of unfettered mechanisation is not socially acceptable since coir production is the major source of employment after agriculture in the coastal tracts. However, at the same time it suggests technology choice for reducing the period of retting, mechanisation of fibre extraction and spinning process.

Karunakaran (1945) examined the various aspects of the problems of coir workers and coir industry and in the report stressed the necessity for organising the coir industry on co-perative basis. The study clarified that for many years in the past attention of the Government was particularly on finding a solution to the disorganized state of affairs that existed in the coir industry of the state in general and the resultant disasters on the labour class in particular. This report laid the foundation for co-operativisation of coir industry in the state.

Smith (1949) made a study on the feasibility of organising the coir industry on co-operative basis and underlined the need for re-organisation of coir industry on co-operative basis. On the basis of the report of the Smith Committee, the erstwhile Govt. of Cochin attempted to organize Coir Industry on co-operative lines.

The Coir Board (1955), appointed an Ad Hoc Committee for Coir Yarn, to study problems relating to production, marketing, grading and standardization of coir yam, role of co-operative organization in coir marketing, role of producers [small and large-scale], method of spinning, production and labour conditions. Though the Committee could not go deep into the all aspects mentioned above, it recommended various measures for the development of the coir sector. The recommendations related to arrangement for a census and registration of spindles, participation of only licensed dealers in the coir trade, popularization of spindle-spinning in Malabar and implementation of Minimum Wages in the Malabar area which was then a part of the then Madras State.

Theyyunni Menon (1959) critically evaluated the functioning of various types of coir societies in the state. His report threw light on the various malpractices connected with this sector. He highlighted the fact that co operatives failed to gain any hold on the industry. The causes responsible for this, according to him, were drawback in the accounting system, administrative delays and multiplicity of societies. The Report suggested various measures to attract coir workers into coir co-operative fold, and stressed the necessity for appointing qualified secretaries for coir societies. A change in the audit system prevailing coir co-operative system was also recommended.

The Coir Board has published two reports; one in 1960 and the other in1962. The 1960 Report was the outcome of an in-depth survey of number of coir households in Kerala. The survey covered aspects relating to occupational status, job satisfaction level, land owned, demographic particulars, income and expenditure of hand-spinning households etc. It also covered spindle-spinning sector in the Kanyakumari district of the then Madras state. The objectives of the survey were to study the socio-economic conditions of the people engaged in the industry, to estimate the total production of coir yarn and consumption of raw material and the total number of households and persons engaged in the industry. It also covered the manufacturing units in registered and unregistered sectors. The report contained several recommendations for the upliftment of the coir sector. But the report had not made an attempt to analyse the Co operativisation Scheme of coir sector in India.

The 1962 report was based on information collected about husk retters' allover Kerala and Kanyakumari district of the then Madras state. It covered the number of workers involved in retting activity in various areas on the basis of variety of yarn production and spindle-spinning. The report made the inference that, considering its contribution towards exports of the country, the importance of the coir sector cannot be ignored. It also stressed the need for diversifying this industry. But the study did not make any attempt to analyze the role of Cooperatives for the development of coir sector in the country

A Task Force was appointed by the Planning Commission under the chairmanship of M.K.K. Nayar (1973) for evaluating the various types of assistance extended to coir industry and coir co-operatives during the fourth Five-year Plan. Basically the Task Force was intended to suggest suitable measures for co-ordinating the development programmes for the coir industry and for making a proposal for the fifth Five-year Plan. The Committee covered all states producing coir and coir products in India and submitted its report. The report identified the importance of Research and Development, modernization, and mechanization in this sector. It also found out various other uses of coir products. But this report failed to give concrete suggestions for solving the problems connected with coir workers and coir co-operatives. However, the Task Force proposed some financial support to the coir sector during the fifth five year plan.

The report on mechanization in coir industry in Kerala brought out by the government of Kerala (1973) identified the relevance of coir industry in Kerala to national economy. The report contained information regarding the structure of coir industry, wage structure, export of coir and coir products from India, internal market of coir products etc. It emphasized the necessity of research and development effort in coir sector so as to modernize it. The report also admitted the sensitiveness of the issue of mechanization of coir production and assessed its problems and possibilities. The report stressed that without modernisation, India cannot produce attractive coir products with modern designs, and hence she may not be able to maintain even her present share of the international market. The report contained several recommendations for the revival of the industry. The most important among them is that co-operatives in these sectors have to be strengthened and mechanisation should be carried out in such a manner that none should be thrown out of employment.

Nair (1977) Committee, in its report entitled "Coir Industry—a study of its structure and organisation with particular reference to employment in Kerala," has touched all areas of the coir industry. Classification of various types of societies, problems of these societies relating to raw material shortage, working capital shortage etc. of Coir Co-operatives, effectiveness of Regulatory measures, estimate about employment, income from coir work and non-coir work, expenditure etc. of coir workers were discussed and analysed by the Committee. On the basis of this the Committee concluded that the performance of the co operative sector was not encouraging. According to the Committee the employment provided by these societies cannot be justified *pari pasu* with the cost involved. The committee further suggested that the Kerala State Coir Corporation should take up the responsibility of distributing the orders received from exporters to small producers and supply yarn and other raw materials at economic cost to them and also provide common services like quality control, dyeing drying etc., for eliminating the middle-men who expropriate the surpluses.

Even though the committee made a sincere attempt to study the problems of this sector, the committee failed to identify the causes for the weak performance of coir co-operatives in Kerala.

The High Powered Study Team under the leadership of B. Sivaraman (1978) found out that, even after the enactment of the Coconut Husk Control Order the co-operatives could not succeed in the field due to non-availability of the required husk for their operations. On the basis of its findings the Committee urged the central and state governments to extend financial help to coir societies to implement the Coir Development Programme.

Kerala State Planning Board (1984) analysed coir industry as a part of studying various traditional industries in Kerala. It went through the structure of coir industry and made an all-India view about employment in coir industry, production of coir products, out-lay and expenditure in coir industry during the five year plans, progress of co-operativisation in coir sector, various Govt. regulations in coir industry including prohibiting the use of defibering machinery etc. It also gave an account of the export statistics of various coir products from 1960-61 to1982-83. The committee put forward some major recommendations for the upliftment of the coir industry. The most important recommendation of the Committee related to prohibition of women working in defibering and retting operations and standardisation of coir yarn produced in different localities into three or four groups.

Department of Economics and Statistics (1986) conducted a study on production and consumption of coir and coir products in Kerala. The study also examined the potential of coir production in other states in India. Production and consumption, nature of coir, employment in this sector, units engaged inorganised and unorganised sector in various activities of coir work etc. were also assessed. The report also analysed distribution of workers in the coir producing units, nature of employment, classification of coir workers as regular wage paid employees and unpaid family workers and distribution of units according to the number of hours worked per day. The study revealed that, the coir industry still continues with unpaid family workers which constituted about 72 per cent of the total workers in the industry and there were considerable under-employment in the industry and the workers were getting only less than 181 days of work in a year. It also revealed that there is considerable under-utilization of equipment due to lack of raw material at a reasonable price.

State Planning Board (1990) appointed a Special Task Force headed by M. Thomas Issac. The Task Force examined the probable measures for increasing the economic availability of husk at reasonable price to coir vyavasaya co-operative societies in Kerala. It also analysed the performance of coir vyavasaya co-operative societies with special reference to export promotion and development of internal market of coir products. The report recognised some priority areas for Research and Development of which the important areas were development of treadle ratt, motorised coir spinning machine, semi automatic looms for weaving etc. But most of the suggestions were of repetitive in nature which could not bring any special advantage to policy makers in dealing with the problem of coir industry.

Coir Board (1990) in its survey report provided a detailed account of the coir industry in Andhra Pradesh. Details like coir fibre production, equipments used in coir production, employment, wages paid to coir workers, and the number of coir co-operatives functioning in that state were also provided. The study also highlighted, occupational status, social status, working hours and number of days worked, wages paid income distribution of coir workers and capital investment in coir industry in the state. The study revealed that 58 per cent of the total coir workers were women and children constituted five percent.

Even though the survey covered coir co-operatives, it failed to give any detailed information regarding their working. The High Power Committee appointed by government of Kerala (1993) under the chairmanship of Thachadi Prabhakaran, made an in-depth study about the working of coir societies in the State. It developed a formula to category sector co-operatives in to A, Band C. It developed a formula for finding out the number of man-days provided by coir societies on the basis of its production.

The study also developed and adopted several criteria for evaluating the working of coir co-operatives in the State. It used a tool for collecting evidences about the drawbacks in working of coir co-operatives and suggestions from the public who were associated with coir co-operatives. But the report failed to suggest any policy for developing the weak societies or for the revival of sick coir societies.

Coir Board (1994) published a report on the coir industry in TamilNadu. This gives a detailed account of coconut production, status of coir industry, number of coir co-operative societies functioning, employment, production of coir, capital investment etc. in Tamil Nadu. The study also revealed the presence of child labour in coir industry. According to the study children accounted for 12 per cent and women, 49 per cent of the total coir workers. The study further showed that income in the coir co-operative sector is less than in the other organised sector. Even though the survey covered coir co operatives, its scope was limited to ascertaining the total number and their membership. So it did not touch upon the detailed working of coir co-operatives in the State.

The committee headed by Anandan (1997) also examined the problems of coir vyavasaya societies in Kerala. The report made a category-wise analysis of the coir society in Kerala. But the report presented only a general picture on issues like share capital, assets, liabilities of coir societies in each category. The report did not highlight any particular merit with respect to any category of the societies. The study also failed in identifying the exact cause of failure of coir societies in the state. In spite of these shortcomings the report contained several recommendations for the upliftment of the coir co-operative sector. The major ones among them were:-

- The dues of the societies to the government should be converted into shares,
- Government should stand as surety for the loans taken by coir co operatives, and

- The Govt. should appoint a committee to study the existing poor service conditions of employees of the coir societies.

Kerala Statistical Institute (1997) conducted a survey on coir industry in Kerala. The report gives deep insight on matters relating to the number of coir workers in the state, coir households, quantity of production of yam, fibre, consumption of fibre, socio-economic aspects of workers in the coir industry in Kerala, etc. The report also gives a picture of the demand for fibre, yam and coir products, its movement from Kerala, and various traditional and non-traditional equipments applied in the industry. The study further revealed that the under utilisation is more discernible in the co-operative sector where more than 50 per cent of under utilisation of equipment was reported. But it has not given any detailed account of the working of coir co-operatives in Kerala.

Vimal (1976), described various uses of Coconut pith, which was considered to be a waste. The areas where this can be used include building industry, manufacture of gasket, agriculture, storage batteries, electroplating, and in rubber compounding. The divergent uses of pith which was considered as a waste material holds great potential.

Alexander (1976) unveiled the economic and social importance of coir industry in India. According to him no cottage industry in Kerala engages so many people in manufacture and trade as in coir industry. He opined that maintenance of a uniform quality is the most important factor in stabilizing and improving exports and the only way to achieve this is through evolving suitable standards for different types of products and ensuring that export conforms strictly to these quality standards. He stressed the necessity of introducing mechanical spinning and defibering from unretted husk in India. He emphasised the importance of diversification and modernization of coir products and hoped the Coir Development Scheme could ameliorate the conditions of workers in societies and the necessity of expanding domestic market for the development of coir industry. The author also claimed that Indian coir yarn has good reputation in the foreign markets and there is a tendency of preferring natural fibres to artificial fibres. He also accepts the complexity of the problems of coir as it vitally concerns the lives of tens of thousands of people while it is an industry with great potential for export as well as for internal consumption. He concluded the article stating that as long as coconut palms tower high in the coastal belt of Kerala the coir industry can exist in the country.

Kunhikrishnan (1977), in his article examines the historical relevance of the coconut tree and its various uses. He also mentions that classical literature of India has glorified coconut tree as 'DevaVkrisha ' or Godly tree as it provides a variety of products useful to daily life. The name of the state 'Keralam'itself comes from coconut, Kera + elam [Kera =coconut, elam =land]. It is stated that research conducted so far shows that coconut is ideally suited for a balanced plant—animal—human eco-system in which perfect harmony between these three life patterns can be achieved to their natural advantage. The coconut growing areas are characterised by a high density of population and so this crop is a boon to the small farmer.

Economic Review (1978) of Kerala, while mentioning different traditional industries in Kerala, states that, when coir co-operatives have started to give reasonable wages, the private coir producers have also been forced to hike the wages. It also advocates various control measures in the industry enforced by Coir Directorate.

Economic Review (1980) highlights that as this industry is a highly labour intensive one, any attempt of modernisation will bring labour displacement. What is required is the expansion of external and internal market, which will add a new dimension to the development of coir industry.

Robin (1984) in his article narrates the historical background of coir industry, features of labour movement in this sector of Kerala state etc. The article throws light on the caste system that prevails in the Kerala society and how it decays the society and the coir workers. The role and influence of 'rnoopan' among coir workers is also touched in the article. He also tries to link the labour movement [their militancy and stamina] in coir industry with Punnapra—Vayalar Revolt in 1946 in Kerala.

Chacko & Parameshwaran Nair (1995) has explained in an article, the steps taken by central and state governments for renovation of coir industry in Kerala and recommended various measures for the welfare of coir workers.

Thomas Isaac (1984) in his work gives a picture of labour movement in coir industrial scene of Kerala from 1859 to 1980. His study throws light on the activities of trade union movements among coir workers and explains how it helped to uplift the coir workers and to reduce their exploitation by middlemen. The work also helps to get an insight into the labour movement in coir industry and how it was linked with the freedom struggle of India. He concluded his work stating that the labour unions were pledged to fight against any move to mechnise the industry without guaranteeing alternative jobs for the displaced workers. The agitation against the machine assumed a new momentum in the mid-seventies. But the study does not focus on the role of formal institutional arrangements like co-operatives for the development of coir workers and coir industry in the State.

Neena (1999) in her dissertation examines the working conditions of women workers in the unorganized sector. She, along with portraying the geographical peculiarity of coir industrial area, types of coir yarn, and the hazardous nature of coir work, also examines the social problems connected with coir work and the suffering of women coir workers in the state. The study found out that, coir workers enjoy very low status in the society and the majority of them belong to a particular community and the economic necessity compelled young women coir spinners to engage in this work and work for 8—10 hours per day. It also adds that in the unorganised sector women workers are preyed upon by contractors and middlemen who exploit their ignorance.

Dhanya (1999), in her report on the problems of women workers in coir industry, focuses on the lifestyle and social conditions of women workers in coir industry. It analyses the socio-economic profile, health problems, and the nature and status of women coir workers. The study reveals the demographic picture of the workers that they were illiterate in most cases. Moreover hard and irregular employments are common features coir industry. The study comes to a conclusion that the improvement of the conditions of coir workers should be the main considerations while thinking about improvement in coir sector and also adds that co-operative sector in coir industry should be revitalized with sufficient funds so as to benefit coir workers too.

Studies on the ecosystem of Cochin backwaters in the retting and non-retting areas were carried out by various authors. Organic matter showed enrichment in the retting ground sediments. Annual average of bacterial biomass was higher in the reference (control) station. Bacterial contribution to total organics was consistently higher at the reference station (Remani et al., 1981).

Fluctuations in the abundance of Crustaceans, the important component of plankton community and a major food item of many fishes in the retting zone were studied. The existence of sulphide system in the retting zone and the seasonal variation in abundance of the Crustacean fauna, in comparison with the non—retting area were discussed by Abdul Aziz et al., 1982.

Environmental pollution due to retting of coconut husk and preliminary studies on closed system retting has been studied by Abbassi, et al., 1982.The retting of coconut husks in the backwaters is brought about by the pectinolytic activity of microorganisms, especially bacteria and fungi, degrading the fibre-binding material of the husk and liberating large quantities of organic substances including pectin, pentosan, fat and tannin into the ambient water.

Microbiological studies of a few coconut retting areas were carried out by Jayasankar & Menon, (1961). Retting activities carried out in anaerobic system were studied by Bhatt, (1969). Effects of retting on water quality and ecosystem of the estuaries of Kerala has been studied in detail by various scientists.

The impact of retting on the fishery wealth was studied by Abdul Azis and Balakrishnan Nair,(1978). Oxidation of organic matter liberates hydrogen sulphide, adversely affecting the fishery wealth of the area. The nature, significance and consequences of this man-made sulphide system were examined in detail and its effect on the fishery of the area was discussed. Fluctuation in the abundance of Crustaceans has a direct bearing on fisheries. The Edava-Nadayara—Paravur backwater system with the exception of the retting areas supports a rich fishery.

Seasonal variations in the Crustacean plankton population with reference to the non-retting areas were noticed by Abdul Aziz, et al., 1982. The existence of sulphide system in the retting zone and the seasonal variation in abundance of the Crustacean fauna in comparison with the non retting area are discussed in detail.

Remani, et al., (1981) studied the characteristics of a retting yard and a control station (reference station) in Cochin backwater. Effects of monsoon were found significant. Organic carbon and organic matter showed enrichment in the retting ground sediments. The C/N ratios were constituently higher in the retting yard. Annual average of bacterial biomass was higher in the non retting yard (25.7mg/g) as against 22.8 mg/g in the retting yard.

Ecology of the Akathumuri, Anjengo and Kadinamkulam lakes and its physicochemical conditions were studied by Balakrishnan Nair.N., (1983) Meiofauna of Edava—Nadayara backwater system, south-west coast of India was studied. Ecology and distribution of benthic macrofauna in the Ashtamudi estuary of Kerala were attempted by Balakrishnan Nair. N. et al., (1984).

Pollution in Cochin backwaters due to coconut husk retting with special reference to benthos, was studied by Remani (1979).Ecology of Vaduthala retting yards in cochin backwaters and its effect on water quality, sediments and estuarine communities, especially local fisheries were reported by Remani et al., (1980). Studies on the sediments of retting yards with reference to the nutrient contents in Cochin backwaters were attempted (Remani et al., 1981). Indicator organisms among benthic communities which dominated maintaining high population densities in retting yards of Cochin backwaters were studied (Remani, et al., 1983).

Various species of Polychaetes which are pollution tolerant are abundantly seen in the retting yards. Studies on the variations of Polychaete fauna in areas affected by retting was attempted by Antony et al., (1982).

Effect of retting on the reproductive potential of green mussel Perna viridis in the intertidal mussel beds of Elathur along the Malabar coast was studied (Ajith Kumar et al., 1982).

Remani & Nirmala (1989) classified the retting yards based on hydrology, area and intensity of retting activities. The process of retting is found to cause pollution problems in the river mouths and backwaters. Detailed systematic studies were carried out in Kadalundi retting yards. Adverse effects of pollution are well marked on the local fishery of these areas.

Assessment of pollution due to retting of coconut husk and development of Alternative Retting Technology was carried out by Remani& Nirmala, 1989, (CWRDM Report). Experiments on the development of alternative retting technology reveals that retting can be practised in fresh water. The periodicity of retting is prolonged in closed system in anaerobic conditions. Flushing of ret liquor reduces the periodicity of retting without affecting the quality of fibre.

Impact of retting industry on the fauna and flora of the backwater system was studied by Remani & Nirmala,

(1990). Correlative assessment of benthic communities in the retting yards based on the taxa and ranges of Dissolved Oxygen content were carried out by Remani & Nirmala, (1989). The high population density and species richness which are the structural parameters of the benthic community suggests a relationship between community composition and dissolved oxygen regime. Acute drinking water scarcity problem is being experienced by the people living in Mannoor area, near Kadalundi. Eighty families requested the Panchayat President, Kadalundi to provide them with safe drinking water (Malayala Manorama, 18thMay 2000).

People who earn their living from retting industry suffer much due to the very low wages they receive from the Coir Mill owners. Thus, low wages compounded with untiring labour and seasonal employment aggravates their poverty (Mathrubhumi, 14th May 2000). Coir workers of Malappuram district in Kerala, is of the opinion that mechanical defibering have lost the job opportunities of many workers who are engaged in this industry (Mathrubhumi, 26th May 2000).

Coir fed has taken the initiative to help the coir industry to achieve new standards of excellence in quality by setting up a Raw Material Bank. Its aim is to ensure uniform high quality of the raw materials required including dyes and chemicals. Today, Coirfed, the apex body of more than 600 co-operative Coir Societies has taken on the mantle of keeping alive this eco-friendly heritage in this land of coconuts. The prosperity of more than four lakh coir workers in its vast family, is ensured directly by Coirfed, while 20 million is benefitted indirectly. (The Hindu, Friday, August 4, 2000)In the traditional retting process, 9-11 months are required for retting the husk, which is a negative factor for the progress of this industry. Central Institute of Alleppy has designed a new methodology for retting the coconut husk within 3 months. A group of bacteria named as "Coir Rett" when introduced @ 6 kg/one tonne coconut husk, can degrade the husk within 3 months. This methodology can be successfully applied for getting 'Golden Fibre' within short duration. This is also an easy way of reducing the pollution load in the retting yard (Mathrubhumi, September 22nd, 1999)

Coir retting yards are concentrated along the southern coastal line and specially women folk; find this work as the source of their principal income for the family in off seasons of fishing. The study was conducted in the Dickwella secretariat division to study the impact of coir retting on the socio-economic and health status of fisher women involved in coir retting. Random sample of 35 coir retting women involved in coir retting was selected. The necessary data of the location and families were collected by using questionnaires, interviews and discussions. Data obtained were statistically analyzed by using Statistical Package for Social Science (SPSS) software. Water quality parameters, such as pH, temperature, BOD, COD, NO_3^-–N and conductivity were analyzed. All the water quality parameters were not in permissible ranges. The average household size and daily net income of the coir retting families involved were 4.5 and Rs. 612.50, respectively. Eighty nine percent has obtained primary education while 9 % and 2 % have gained secondary and tertiary education respectively. It is obvious that these people do not have any access to other employment opportunities except coir retting due to lack of education. The results revealed that the coir retting industry of this area is an activity that is intricately interwoven with the social and economic structure. Field survey results indicated that 57 % of the sample suffered from job-oriented disease like skin disease, blindness, headache, back bone pains and respiratory disease. Rotted husk release more organic pollutants and they highly affect the water quality parameters. Therefore, it is a difficult task to save these women from these occupational hazards unless some new affordable technique is introduced. Majority of the households (70 %) fall within a low socio-economic status with a deepening poverty background depicted by low educational achievement and occupational status.

CHAPTER IV

The Design Framework for Multimedia

4.1 INTRODUCTION

This chapter explains the design and development of a multimedia package. In the development of the material attention has been paid to the accommodation of multimedia learning principles and instructional design principles.

To create an innovative interactive multimedia application, a multimedia designer needs to rapidly explore numerous design ideas early in the design process, as creating an innovative design is the corner stone of creating an innovative multimedia learning platform. On reviewing the literature related to Cognitive theory and multimedia learning principles, instructional design and ADDIE model, the investigator is trying to design and develop a multimedia package based on the integrated design principles derived from the multimedia learning principles with the help of ADDIE instructional design model.

The ADDIE (Analysis, Design, Development, Implementation, Evaluation) model adopted for this research study is possibly the best known design model(Siemens, 2002; Driscoll, 1998) and further this instructional design model is a practical generic model which is easily implemented (Piskurich, Beckesci & Hall, 2000; Malachowski, 2002).

The chapter begins with an overview of the design process of the multimedia learning package and then the design for innovation and intervention in the teaching and learning process is discussed. Finally the integration of the ADDIE model of instructional design into the process of the design and the development of the interactive multimedia package is discussed and described.

4.2 THE DESIGN PROCESS OF A MULTIMEDIA PACKAGE

The design of the curricular content forces the researcher to make choices, hypotheses and expectations explicit. Inherent in the development of the design is the potential for a shift in theoretical emphasis as the researcher's insights and hypotheses develop (Bakker, Doorman & Drijvers, 2003). Dogan & Walker (2002) believe that the designer is able both to achieve an 'integrated approach' and to demonstrate the effectiveness of this approach. This in turn will affect the researcher's overall method in the design context: It is the design that demonstrates the inherent value of the product. Edelson (2002) argues that the "design process "is a meaningful part of the research methodology employed.

The design process and the development of any curricular content happen within a particular contextual situation: a designer of real world applications should therefore try to describe the context in which they will be used (Levy, 1997) as possibly accurately as possible, and an explicit statement of the learning environment should be made (Johnson & Brine, 2000). There are several main components of the learning environment. The first of these is the learning or teaching method used (Hubbard, 1987): then there is the learning situation co-operative or individual. The next part of the environment is the curriculum, identified either in terms of the proficiency guidelines (Egan, 1999) or as institutional/instructional goals (Meskill, 1991; Field, 2002). Lastly, there are technological considerations regarding knowledge both of the strengths and limitations available courseware and of the strengths and limitations of the technologies (Fox, 1997; Egan, 1999). These considerations may include development environments, electronic learning environments (Goodfellow, 1999), operating systems and networking technologies (Colpaert, 2004). Developing prototype is an integral part of an iterative user-centred design process because it enables designers to try out their ideas with real users and to gather feedback on design issues (Shin & Wastell, 2001). According to Meskill (1991) & Hubbard (1992), the design process is not only a process of 'simultaneously considering, juggling and reconciling a number of issues", it is also a balancing act between theory and practice theory and technology (Levy, 1999; Hemard & Cushion, 2000).

Colpaert (2004) points out that the main challenge for designers is to come to grips with the design process, sorting through all of the factors to be considered in making a decision about the best line of attack. One way of managing the rather disparate elements involved in the process is for the designer or the developer is to bridge the gap between "the learner's domain or specificity requirements and the designer's domain or applicability requirements" (Hemard, 1998).This leads to a discussion of the design for innovation and intervention in the teaching and learning process.

4.3 INTEGRATION OF THE ADDIE MODEL OF INSTRUCTIONAL DESIGN IN THE DESIGN AND DEVELOPMENT OF THE MULTIMEDIA PACKAGE.

The ADDIE generic model of instructional design is used in the development of the multimedia learning package. Each phase of the model delivers output which serves as the input for subsequent phases. ADDIE is an instructional design model which is valid for any kind of education and despite the fact that ADDIE comprises the components of all other design models it is a relatively simple model.

A model does not automatically fit into every research investigation: rather each model can be adjusted to a particular research methodology. Sloane & Gorard (2003) argue that model building is largely ignored by novice researchers and suggest therefore general principles for model formulation. The model should in their opinion (i) be the outcome of consultation and discussion with appropriate experts on the given topic, (ii) be formulated on empirical or theoretical grounds that are consistent with any qualitative knowledge of the system and (iii) take into account that all models are approximate and tentative. All the above mentioned principles are consistent with the design methodology of this study.

The next section discusses each phase of ADDIE model in the context of this research study.

4.4 ADDIE FRAMEWORK FOR THE DEVELOPMENT OF MULTI-MEDIA PACKAGE

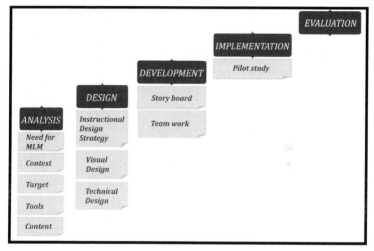

Fig. 4.1 ADDIE Framework for the development of Multimedia Package

The framework focuses on the five stages—Analysis, Design, Development, Implementation and Evaluation. It captures the major inputs and processes within each of these stages, defines the outcomes for all the inputs and sub-processes. This framework provides a sound base for the development of multimedia package.

4.4.1 The Analysis Phase

This step is the description process of what is going to be taught and forms the basis of all other steps. In this step, the designer determines the needs and the difference between knowledge, skills and behaviours, which the learners presently have, and behaviours which they must have or they are expected to have. Prior to developing any Multi-Media Learning Materials several questions—relating to the target audience, the nature of Multi-Media Learning Material, the learning styles, the conditions under which utilized, the purpose for the Multi-Media Material and the nature of the content—need to be answered. Unless there is clarity on these and several related issues the compatibility between the Multi-Media Learning Material and the learner may not be achieved. Analysis hence should capture the requirements and set expectations of the Multi-Media Material. A study of analysis may be carried under five heads: needs, context, target group, task and content. These analyses would provide important inputs into design, development, implementation and assessment considerations.

❖ *Need for Multi-Media Package*

The first step is to identify the needs from the perspective of different stakeholders. A survey was conducted by the student teachers of Sree Narayana Training College on the socio economic as well as health status of women coir workers of Anchuthengu panchayath. They found the need for an awareness campaign regarding the occupational diseases and health hazards for the target group. From review it was found that no readymade multimedia materials are available to ensure awareness to them. Hence there arises a need to design and develop a multimedia package based on health awareness.

❖ *Context*

The context is clearly and fully mapped. The data regarding contextual variables such as learning environment is collected which include whether the target group is an individual or group. It may also specify whether the learning environment is formal or informal, facilitated or self learning. Information regarding technical as well as internet facilities are mentioned.

❖ *Target Group*

In the third step the investigator collected data regarding the learning group that includes their academic level and attribute like skills, motivation, visual literacy, language competency, learning styles etc. The learning styles include visual style (learning by seeing), auditory style (learning by hearing) and kinesthetic style (learning by doing). The learning groups are women coir workers of coastal areas of Kerala.

❖ *Task*

This step entitles the investigator to clearly state the purpose and to identify the usage aspects of the multimedia material. The purposes may include education, training, enrichment, awareness, skill development or any other. The investigator tries to infuse most of the purposes such as education, enrichment, and skill development etc as the primary purpose of the multimedia material. The usage aspects of MLM refers to how the MLM is intended to be used whether as a self-sufficient module or in accompaniment with other print and non-print modules, whether it is intended for independent use by the learner or with support from facilitators.

❖ *Content*

The final step includes selection, verification and classification of content. The investigator with consultation with expert doctors of medical colleges prepared the material.

4.4.2 Design phase

The design phase considers three sub-processes Instructional Design Strategy, Visual Design and Technical Design. Prototype Testing is included in the Design Phase to make necessary changes before development.

❖ *Instructional Design*

Bailey, Konstan & Carlis (2001) contend that multimedia design focus on creating a unique user experience through the coherent use of attractive content, engaging interaction and time-based information display. It is always useful to keep in mind that the content should drive the course development process (Jones & Frommer, 1999) and it is important to analyse and outline the content to be used. This will assist the instructional designer to list the main concepts, in order to determine sub steps and their relevant details (Hall, 1997). The investigator takes the role of the script writer. The investigator creates character, action and interactivity. The structuring of content in the content map is from simple to complex, known to unknown, concrete to abstract and also general to specific.

❖ *Visual Design*

In addition to the specific content presented in the multimedia package, the design of learning material requires attention to cognitive functioning and overload. Clark & Mayer (2003) note that one of the challenges of multimedia projects "is to build lessons in ways that are compatible with human learning processes. To be effective, instructional methods must support these processes." Mayer's six principles from the cognitive theory of multimedia learning is applied thus guiding the development of effective learning. For example, based on the contiguity principle the words are placed near their corresponding images and instructions near the act. Mayer (2001) proposes that the cognitive theory of multimedia learning addresses the competing nature of the dual channels (auditory and visual) for processing information in the construction of knowledge in contrast to basic information delivery theory which focuses on the methods of delivery (e.g. audio, video, text). In other words, designers want to use the most effective medium for delivery of information and also to balance the demands placed on the learner's auditory and visual channels of communication processing.

With awareness of these cognitive limitations, the investigator incorporated interaction in the form of making decisions, analyzing problems, constructing knowledge, or practicing skills or concepts. The first step here is designing Graphical User Interface (GUI).Graphical User Interface refers to the interface which allows the user to interact with the MLM and the computer screen. i.e. it comprises all the (graphical) navigational features that allow the user to interact with the MLM and browse through it. A visually appealing and intuitive GUI is designed by the investigator.

❖ *Media Selection*

One factor that determines whether multimedia courseware can be effective in enhancing learner's learning is the quality of the software itself: in other words the quality of the design (Greene, 2000; Fox, 1997). Some of the major components of multimedia courseware include the design of multimedia material, interface, navigational structure, communication, orientation and instructional strategies (Goodfellow, 1999; Hemard, 1998). When designers plan multimedia learning environment they should be concerned with "user expertise, personal interest, node content and navigation design" (Wang & Beasley, 2002). The software allows instructional designers, training developers and subject matter expert to develop tractable learning applications and develop them across the Web, LANs and CD-ROM.

4.4.3 The Development Phase

Once the comprehensive and demanding design phase is completed, the development phase commences: the stage that deals with the actual production of the learning materials. The following practical matters are addressed in the development phase: story board development, team work and naming the Multimedia package.

❖ *Development of Storyboard*

One of the important considerations for the Development phase is the preparation of the storyboard. This would be a pre-requisite for any multimedia learning material development. It provides the link between the design phase and the development of the learning package. A story board is an expression of everything that will be contained in the program—what menu screens look like, what pictures(still and moving) will be seen, when and for how long, what audio and text will accompany the images, either synchronously or hyperlinked.

Klaus (2002) points that a story board is a plan for teaching and learning activities and it can combine the outlines and sketches that map out the contents or sequence of ideas. A story board is structured based on objectives and defined instructional strategies. The story board cards are placed in order to provide the foundation for capturing the proper footage and for making the correct editing decisions.

❖ *Team work*

Bannan-Ritland (2003) explains that when the rough outlines for the intervention are apparent, the design team creates a composite depiction, or a sort of a model, for the development of the software environment to the identified needs of the user. Designing multimedia generally requires a team effort because a good result requires many different design skills. We needed instructional design skills to determine the goal of instruction and select instructional strategies and multimedia elements, writing skills to write content, information architecture skills to structure the content so it was easily to follow and access, graphic design skills to develop clear and attractive navigation and explanatory graphics, multimedia skills to work with instructional designers to create interactive elements. That is design and development of a Multimedia package involves the integration of both instructional designing and graphical designing. The instructional designer designs the instruction while the graphic designer gives flesh and blood to the instructional material through graphic designing. During this phase, the instructional designer (investigator) and the professional graphic artist worked closely together with each other to develop the multimedia learning package. The professional graphic artist recreated several diagrams from the existing course materials in digital format.

❖ *Naming the Multimedia Package*

Now the package is ready for implementation. The investigator together with the multimedia development team suggest name for the package developed. Here in the present study the investigator named the multimedia learning package as '*Health Literacy Package*' with due relevance to its content.

4.4.4. The Implementation phase

Implementation means putting the product into action. Learning skills or understanding are "demonstrated to the participants, who practice initially in a safe setting and then in the targeted workplace (Malachowski, 2002; Coalpert, 2004). Within this context the implementation phase was conducted through a pilot study to a small group of women coir workers. Focus group interviews and individual interviews were conducted with them.

4.4.5. The Evaluation phase

Evaluation can be defined as the process of making judgments regarding the appropriateness of some person, program, process, or product for a specific purpose (Shrock & Coscarelli, 2000). "Evaluation examines the effectiveness of the instruction by considering how well the outcomes, assessments, and activities are aligned within the instruction and whether they are appropriate for the needs and characteristics of the learners" (Cennamo & Kalk, 2005). Evaluation involves formative evaluation and summative evaluation. The formative evaluation stage is where each prototype of the product will be evaluated by the target audience (users) and experts. These evaluations are necessary for revisions and modifications that may be needed to ensure that the finished product meets its overall objectives. Formative evaluation is done through observations, interviews, surveys, and records (Dick & Carey, 1991).The summative evaluation stage is where the finished product is tested by the target audience to validate its effectiveness.

CHAPTER V

Awareness Programme on Occupational Diseases

5.1 INTRODUCTION

Health promotion is the process of enabling people to increase control over, and to improve, their health. To reach a state of complete physical, mental and social well-being, an individual or group must be aware of various health hazards and the importance of hygiene. Most of the inhabitants in coastal areas are illiterates. Multimedia health promotion campaigns can be used to educate the public about health issues with the aim of influencing women to change their lifestyle. Health promotion is not just the responsibility of the health sector alone, but is the responsibility of each individual. A teacher being a social engineer is responsible to the whole society. Teachers should try to develop health awareness to students as well as community. This project enabled to have a close link with the community with a goal to promote health and well being among individuals, communities and populations, enabling them to address the broad determinants of health in order to reduce the vulnerability and risks to ill health and disability throughout the life cycle, especially among women. Due to lack of time and the nature of the course, the investigator limited her study within the Anjengo panchayat. The awareness programme with the help of the multimedia package started with the following hypotheses.

HYPOTHESES

The hypotheses of the study are

1. The women coir workers are unaware of the various occupational diseases, its health hazards and various remedial measures.
2. The developed multimedia learning package is effective in enhancing the health awareness level regarding occupational diseases among the women coir workers.

OBJECTIVES OF THE STUDY

- To study the impact of coir retting on the health status of the women, with special reference to those employed in this trade.
- To develop multimedia packages on 'health education for women' with special reference to occupational diseases.
- To conduct 'Awareness Campaign' with the help of multimedia packages.
- To empower the coastal women engaged in coir retting regarding health.

METHODOLOGY

The methodology employed to collect relevant quantitative & qualitative data needed for the present study is done under the following steps.

- Preliminary survey of the retting yards regarding awareness level on occupational diseases, its health hazard and remedial measures among the women coir workers of Anjengo Panchayat.
- Conducting awareness campaigns by the student teachers with the help of the developed multimedia package.
- Collaborating with other local bodies such as panchayats, blocks and health centers to promote health education.

TOOLS AND TECHNIQUES USED IN THE STUDY

- Occupational Disease Awareness inventory
- Multimedia-learning Package based on Health awareness of occupational disease related to coir retting
- Questionnaire to analyze the extent of health awareness regarding occupational disease related to coir industry.

The present study was intended to investigate the effectiveness of a health education multimedia Package used for health awareness for the women workers engaged in coir industry. This plurality of process calls for multiple methodologies which include both Survey and

Experiment. Hence, it was decided to divide this chapter into two sections.

Descriptive section: *For analyzing existing awareness level of women coir workers on the occupational diseases, its health hazards and various remedial measures.*

Experimental section: *For assessing the effectiveness of developed Multimedia Package*

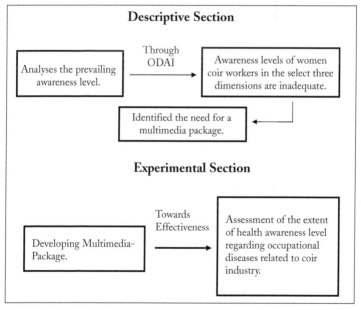

Descriptive Section

Analyses the prevailing awareness level. → Through ODAI → Awareness levels of women coir workers in the select three dimensions are inadequate.

Identified the need for a multimedia package. ←

Experimental Section

Developing Multimedia-Package. → Towards Effectiveness → Assessment of the extent of health awareness level regarding occupational diseases related to coir industry.

Fig. 5.1: RESEARCH DESIGN

The details of the method used, tools and techniques employed, sample selected and the respective mode of analysis are stated separately for each phase. The design of the investigation is given in Fig. 5.1.

5.2.1 Descriptive Section

Descriptive research is concerned with the current status of something. This type of research describes the existing achievement, attitudes, behaviour or other characteristics of a group of subjects. A descriptive study asks what is; it reports things the way they are. Descriptive research is concerned primarily with the present and does not involve manipulation of independent variables (Macmillan and Schumacher, 1989).

Survey was the method used in this section of the study. An occupational disease awareness inventory was used to collect data. It was conducted to find out the existing awareness level of women coir workers regarding occupational diseases and its health hazards.

5.2.2 Experimental Section

Experimental research provides a systematic and logical method answering the question, "If this is done under carefully controlled conditions, what will happen?"

Since the main objective of the present study was to design and try out of a multimedia learning material for heath education, the experimental method was adopted for the study. Experimental design is the blueprint of the procedures that enable the researcher to test hypotheses by reaching valid conclusions about relationships between independent and dependent variables. Selection of a particular design is based upon the purposes of the conditions or limiting factors under which it is conducted (Best 1996). The adequacy of experimental designs is judged by the degree to which the eliminate or minimize threats to experimental validity.

In conducting the experiment for the study, the design adopted was single group pre-test post-test design.

5.3 TOOLS USED IN THE STUDY

The tools used in the present study are

5.3.1 Multimedia Package based on Health awareness of occupational disease related to coir retting.

A health awareness multimedia package was developed as an instructional treatment (See Chapter—IV). The instructional material in the multimedia learning package consists of occupational health hazards due to coir retting and its preventive measures.

The structure of multimedia package has been designed in such a way that it can address the requirements of the user. The screen snap shots of some of the scenes are shown below.

5.3.2 Occupational Disease Awareness inventory

The term 'inventory' is applied to devices which aid the researcher in studying the interests, attitudes and personality of his target group. Inventories help in analysing many factors influencing societal work and developing remedial procedures. In this study, the researcher had to specify the essential preventive measures and to identify the extent of prevailing health awareness level with a view to develop multimedia learning package for effective health awareness and subsequently organising an awareness campaign based on the prepared package on the women coir workers. This inventory is meant to highlight the need of the multimedia package for the coir retting women along the coastal areas of Kerala.

. The inventory used in the study is based on health education under the select three dimensions

a) Extend of awareness on job related diseases
b) Extent of awareness on health hazards of job related diseases
c) Extent of awareness on remedial measures

5.3.3 Questionnaire to analyze the extent of health awareness regarding occupational disease related to coir industry.

A questionnaire was prepared by the investigator to assess the awareness level of women coir workers regarding the health hazards of related works in coir industry.

5.4 SAMPLE SELECTED

Sampling is fundamental in any form of research intending to draw a generalization for specified population. According to Cornell (1960) the term sampling stands for the process by which a relatively small number of individuals or measures of individuals, objects or events is selected or analysed in order to find out something about the entire population or universe from which it was selected. Selection of sample should be based upon the purpose of investigation. A suitable sample of coir workers of Anchuthengu panchayath is selected. Random sampling method was used.

5.5 PROCEDURE ADOPTED IN EXPERIMENTATION

The experiment was conducted to study the effectiveness of the developed multimedia Package for enhancing the awareness level of women coir workers on occupational diseases and its remedial measures. The procedure adopted in conducting the experiment is given below.

1) Survey on the awareness level
2) Pre-test conducted
3) Awareness campaign to the experimental group with the help of Multimedia Package
4) Post-test conducted

5.5.1 Pre-test Conducted

Before starting the experiment, the investigator administered the prepared Questionnaire to analyze the extent of health awareness regarding occupational disease related to coir industry to the target group. In the administration of the test, the investigator personally read the questions for the target group. The scores thus obtained were used for statistical analysis.

5.5.2 Awareness campaign to the Target Group with the help of multimedia learning package

Awareness campaign is an effective way of communication to the mass, since such programmes are highly relevant in transferring research / extension / management aspects to the public. Awareness camps were conducted in various Wards of Anchuthengu Panchayat. Through awareness classes target groups were informed and disseminated scientific knowledge about occupational diseases and its control.

The major segment of the rural community, who assembled in the awareness camps conducted in the various Wards of the target sites were women. Through discussions and demonstration classes with the help of multimedia package (Chapter IV), they were educated on the various components related occupational diseases. The multimedia learning package consists of text information ideally supported by graphics which is preferably presented to provide information in an appealing and easily understood manner. Multimedia material was prepared and distributed among the target groups who attended the 'Awareness Camps'.

5.5.3 Post test Conducted

After the completion of awareness campaign post test (Questionnaire to analyze the extent of health awareness regarding occupational disease related to coir industry was conducted by the investigator for the target group. The scores thus obtained were used for statistical analysis.

5.6 STATISTICAL PROCEDURE ADOPTED

To test the tenability of the hypothesis formulated for present study the following statistical technique were employed.

- Percentage Analysis
- Critical ratio

CHAPTER VI

Analysis and Interpretation of Data

This chapter presents the data collected from the survey and the experiment which was subjected to descriptive and inferential analysis. The analysis of data involves breaking down the complex tabulated material into simpler parts and putting them together in new arrangements to determine the inherent meanings and facts.

A critical examination of the results will lead to the acceptance or rejection of the proposed hypotheses that in turn will contribute to knowledge in the particular area. The analysis of data is the heart of the research report. However valid, reliable and adequate the data may be, it does not serve any worthwhile purpose unless it is carefully edited, systematically classified and tabulated, scientifically analysed, intelligently interpreted and rationally concluded. Statistical techniques have contributed greatly in gathering, organising, analysing and interpreting numerical data.

The process of interpretation is essentially one of stating what the results show. Interpretation is not a routine and mechanical process. It calls for a careful, logical and critical examination of the results obtained after analysis, keeping in view the limitations of the sample chosen, the tools selected and used in the study. It is a very important step in the total procedure of research. The study is presented in two sections:

Section I: Extent of awareness on occupational diseases and its remedial measures.

Section II: Effectiveness of the multimedia material for health education among the women coir workers of Anjengo panchayat

6.1 DATA ANLYSIS

6.1.1 SECTION 1: EXTENT OF AWARENESS ON OCCUPATIONAL DISEASES AND ITS REMEDIAL MEASURES.

The objectives which are to be realised in this section are:

1. To find out the extent of awareness on occupational diseases and its remedial measures among the women coir workers of Anjengo panchayat.
2. To develop a multimedia package for providing awareness on health education related to occupational disease due to coir retting.

The extent of occupational health awareness was found out through a survey. An Inventory (constructed and standardised by the investigator) based on health education under the select three dimensions was used to collect relevant data. Ratings of women coir workers were collected; frequency and percentage of responses of the select three dimensions were computed. Details are given in the relevant tables:

6.1.1.1 Ratings of Women Coir Workers Regarding Their Extent of Awareness on Job Related Diseases

In order to find the extent of awareness percentages of responses of the select coir workers were computed. Details are given in Table 6.1.

Dimension	Unaware %	Aware to some extent %	Aware to a certain extent %	Aware to a great extent %	Aware %
Awareness on Job Related Diseases	18.70	57.61	21.80	1.82	0.07

Table 6.1 Responses of Coir Workers Regarding their Awareness on Job Related Diseases

From Table 6.1, it is clear that women coir workers of Anjengo panchayat are unaware of occupational diseases and its effects. As far as the responses in the table were concerned, more than fifty percent (57.61%) don't know about the various occupational as well as communicable diseases and nearly one-fifth (18.70%) of the coir workers know about these diseases to some extent. Almost the same percentage (21.80%) of the coir workers have heard about such diseases and it was also noted that only a negligible percentage of coir workers marked their responses as aware to a great extend (1.82%) and aware (0.07%).

The above responses indicated that almost all the workers selected for the study do not have knowledge on the various occupational diseases. To overcome this problem, specific awareness programmes for enhancing the awareness of workers on various job related diseases need to be designed.

6.1.1.2 Ratings of Women Coir Workers Regarding their Extent of Awareness on Health Hazards of Job Related Diseases

In order to identify the extent of prevailing awareness level of coir workers on the health hazards of occupational diseases the percentages of were computed. The details are given in Table 6.2.

Dimension	Unaware %	Aware to some extent %	Aware to a certain extent %	Aware to a great extent %	Aware %
Awareness on Health Hazards of Job Related Diseases	32.68	43.03	17.96	5.81	0.52

Table 6.2 Responses of Women Coir Workers Regarding their Extent of Awareness on the Health Hazards of Job Related Diseases

The results of Table 6.2 revealed that though the women coir workers are suffering from such diseases they are unable to identify the health hazards of these diseases. While considering the responses of the select sample, majority (43.03%) of the coir workers are unaware of the various health hazards of coir dyes and coir pith while most of the sample selected (32.68%) opined that they are aware of the health hazards to some extent. A small proportion of coir workers (17.96%) are aware of the various effects of occupational diseases to certain extend and a few (5.81%) are aware of it to a great extent. It was also noted that a negligible percentage (0.52%) of coir workers 'are aware of all the health hazards of working in coir industry.

6.1.1.3 Ratings of women coir workers regarding their Extent of awareness on the remedial measures

To find the extent awareness on the remedial the percentages of responses of the select coir workers were computed. The details are given in Table 6.3.

Dimension	Unaware %	Aware to some extent %	Aware to a certain extent %	Aware to a great extent %	Aware %
Awareness on the Remedial Measures	45.85	43.50	10.50	0.15	0.00

Table 6.3 Responses of Women Coir Workers Regarding their Extent of Awareness on the Remedial Measures

While analysing the results obtained from Table 6.3, it was found that nearly half (45.85%) of the selected coir workers are unaware of the remedial measures to avoid occupational diseases to a certain extent, and almost an equal percentage (43.50%) of coir workers are aware of remedial measures only to some extent. Very few coir workers (10.50%) are aware of it to certain extend, while a negligible percentage (0.15%) of coir workers are aware of the remedial measures to a great extent. It was surprisingly noted that none of the coir workers in the select sample are aware of the various remedial measures for occupational diseases.

The alarming percentage of negative responses as per Table 6.3 indicates the urgent need of chalking out an awareness programme to conscientise coir workers about the occupational disease, its effect and various remedial strategies which can be practiced to avoid such job related diseases to certain extend. Hence the investigator decided to design and develop a ready to use package on Health Education to make the women coir workers aware of all the health hazards caused due to their occupation.

6.1.2 SECTION-II: EFFECTIVENESS OF THE MULTIMEDIA PACKAGE

After identifying the areas of awareness needed investigator tried to design and develop a multimedia learning material with the help of a graphical designer. Interviews were conducted with expert doctors in the field.

The main thrust of this section is to identify the effectiveness of the developed multimedia material on

Health Awareness. It was found out through the following mode:

- Extent of awareness on Health education related to occupational disease due to coir retting.

The objective which is to be realized in this section is:

1. To find the effectiveness of developed multimedia package on Health Awareness of Occupational Diseases due to Coir Retting.

To find the effectiveness of the developed multimedia package on Health education related to occupational disease due to coir retting. The investigator compared pre-test and post-test scores of the target groups using t-test. The details are as follows.

6.2.1.1 Comparison of the Pre-test and Post-test Scores of Participants on the Health awareness

The mean and standard deviation of pre-test and post-test scores of the select sample in the experimental group were computed and the effectiveness of multimedia material on awareness of occupational diseases are found out by computing the critical ratio. Table 5.16 presents the data and results of the test of significance.

Test	N	Mean	Standard Deviation	Critical Ratio
Pre-Test	94	20.61	3.53	42.79**
Post-Test	94	60.34	8.28	

** $p<0.01$

Table 6.4 Data and results of the Test of Significance of Difference between the Mean Pre-test and Post-test Scores of the Participants in the Experimental Group

The critical ratio was 42.79. Entering Table D with 186 df, we find that the critical ratios at 0.05 and 0.01 levels were to be 1.97 and 2.80 respectively. The obtained critical ratio was higher than 2.80. Hence, the obtained difference was significant beyond 0.01 levels. This indicates that the pre and post-test on health awareness on occupational diseases of experimental group differed significantly. Since the mean score of the post-test was higher than that of the pre-test, the experimental group performed well in the post-test on health awareness. So, it can be concluded that the multimedia package was effective in enhancing awareness coir workers on the health hazards of occupational diseases and its remedial measures.

6.2 TENABILITY OF HYPOTHESES

The hypotheses formulated for the present study are:

Hypothesis 1

Awareness level of Women coir workers of coastal areas of Kerala on the various health hazards of occupational diseases and its remedial measures are inadequate.

The findings of the study related to this hypothesis throw light on the fact that coir workers of coastal areas of Kerala are unaware of occupational diseases and remedial measures.

When the Occupational diseases Awareness Inventory (ODAI) scores were subjected to statistical analysis following results were arrived at:

a) Only a small percentage of coir workers were found to be aware of various occupational diseases (percentages ranged from 0 to 7.18), while the majority of the coir workers were found to be ignorant about the various occupational as well as communicable diseases (percentages ranged from 10.50 to 57.61-Vide Table 5.1 to 5.5).

b) Majority (43.03%) of the coir workers are unaware of the various health hazards of coir dyes and coir piths while most of the sample selected (32.68%) opined that they are aware of the health hazards to some extent. A small proportion of coir workers (17.96%) are aware of the various effects of occupational diseases to certain extend and a few (5.81%) are aware of it to a great extent. It was also noted that a negligible percentage (0.52%) of coir workers 'are aware of all the health hazards of working in coir industry.

c) While analysing the results it was found that nearly half (45.85%) of the selected coir workers

'Never' practised the remedial measures to avoid occupational diseases to a certain extent, and almost an equal percentage (43.50%) of coir workers'Rarely' practised the same. Very few coir workers (10.50%) 'Sometimes' practised them, while a negligible percentage (0.15%) of coir workers 'Often' practised the remedial measures. It was surprisingly noted that none of the coir workers in the select sample 'Always' practised the various remedial measures,

The above results substantiate the finding that the women coir workers of Anjengo panchayat are unaware of the various occupational diseases its health hazards and its various remedial measures.

Hence, the hypothesis is accepted.

Hypothesis 2

The multimedia package is effective for women coir workers in enhancing awareness of health hazards of occupational diseases and its remedial measures.

The null hypothesis was formulated as:

The multimedia package on health awareness is not effective in enhancing awareness of occupational diseases for coir retting women of coastal areas of Kerala.

This hypothesis was found tenable since findings of the study related to this section favoured the better performance of the experimental group;

When the pre—and post—test scores on health awareness of the experimental group were compared, the critical ratio obtained was found to be significant at 0.01 level (CR = 42.79; p < 0.01).

The above results substantiated the finding that the multimedia-learning package on health awareness of occupational diseases is effective for women coir workers of coastal areas of Kerala. Hence, the hypothesis is proved to be true and tenable and the null hypothesis is summarily rejected.

This study clearly supports the skilful use of Multimedia Packages on Health awareness of occupational diseases for women coir workers of Kerala.

CHAPTER VII

Summary, Conclusions and Recommendations

7.1 INTRODUCTION

This chapter comprises a brief summary of the procedure adopted and the conclusions and suggestions derived from the study.

The present study was mainly intended to design and develop a multimedia package on Health Awareness related to occupational diseases due to coir retting and to provide health awareness among the coir workers of coastal areas of Kerala. As the prelude to the experimental study, the extent of prevailing health awareness regarding occupational diseases and the need of awareness among women coir workers in the select three dimensions of occupational disease awareness were identified with a view to preparing multimedia package

A preliminary analysis of the scores of the different variables was attempted, to answer the research questions posed and tested the hypotheses formulated for the study. The study in retrospect is followed by a short description of the conclusions drawn from the study and a brief summary of the findings. The chapter concludes with implications and practical suggestions on the basis of the findings emerging from of the study.

7.2 CONCLUSIONS BASED ON THE FINDINGS OF THE STUDY

The conclusions that emerged from the results of the analysis of data according to the hypotheses formulated for the study are given under two sections.

Section I: Extent of health awareness on occupational diseases related to coir industry and its remedial measures.

Section II: Effectiveness of the multimedia learning material for health education among the women coir workers of Kerala

Section I: Extent of health awareness on occupational diseases related to coir industry and its remedial measures

The first hypothesis in this section is: The prevailing awareness level of the coir workers on the various health hazards of occupational diseases and its remedial measures are adequate.

It pertains to analysis of the Occupational disease Awareness Inventory score, and the following conclusions were arrived at:

Conclusion 1

The prevailing health awareness level of women coir workers regarding occupational diseases is not satisfactory in all the select three dimensions.

This is supported by the following findings of the study:

d) Only a small percentage of coir workers were found to be aware of various occupational diseases (percentages ranged from 0 to 7.18), while the majority of the coir workers were found to be ignorant about the various occupational as well as communicable diseases (percentages ranged from 10.50 to 57.61-Vide Table 5.1 to 5.5).

e) Majority (43.03%) of the coir workers are unaware of the various health hazards of coir dyes and coir piths while most of the sample selected (32.68%) opined that they are aware of the health hazards to some extent. A small proportion of coir workers (17.96%) are aware of the various effects of occupational diseases to certain extend and a few (5.81%) are aware of it to a great extent. It was also noted that a negligible percentage (0.52%) of coir workers 'are aware of all the health hazards of working in coir industry.

f) While analysing the results it was found that nearly half (45.85%) of the selected coir workers 'Never' practiced the remedial measures to avoid occupational diseases to a certain extent, and almost an equal percentage (43.50%) of coir workers 'Rarely' practiced the same. Very few coir workers (10.50%) 'Sometimes' practised them, while a negligible percentage (0.15%) of coir workers 'Often' practiced the remedial measures. It was surprisingly noted that none of the coir workers in the select sample 'Always' practiced the various remedial measures.

Section II: Effectiveness of the multimedia package for health education among the women coir workers of Kerala

Conclusions from the first section of this chapter reveal that the women coir workers of coastal areas of Kerala are ignorant of the various diseases related to their job. It is found that they do not practice any remedial measures to avoid the health hazards of occupational diseases.

Majority of the women are engaged in retting industry, irrespective of their age. Since they are spending almost the whole day in the unhygienic conditions prevailing in the yard they are at a high risk of developing occupational diseases. Their lack of knowledge about health and hygiene serves as the prime reason for the contagious diseases. From review of related studies it was revealed that the coir retting industry is an activity that is intricately interwoven with the social and economic structure. Field survey results indicated that 57 % of the sample suffered from job-oriented disease like skin disease, blindness, headache, back bone pains and respiratory disease. Rotted husk release more organic pollutants and they highly affect the water quality parameters. Therefore, it is a difficult task to save these women from these occupational hazards unless some new affordable technique is introduced. Majority of the households (70 %) fall within a low socio-economic status with a deepening poverty background depicted by low educational achievement and occupational status. Hence there arise the need to make them aware of the various health hazards, its causes and effects. The search for a strategy which enables to give them awareness regarding health education results in an awareness program through multimedia. Hence, the investigator aims in developing a multimedia package for health and hygiene for coastal women and to conduct awareness program with the help of the developed package on the target group of coir retting industry so as to empower them.

The second hypothesis is: The developed multimedia package is effective in enhancing the health awareness level regarding occupational diseases among the women coir workers.

It is related to the analysis of awareness test on health education regarding occupational diseases related to coir industry. And the following conclusion was emerged.

Conclusion-2

The developed multimedia package is effective in enhancing the health awareness level regarding occupational diseases among the women coir workers.

This conclusion is supported by the following findings

(a) When the pre—and post—test scores on health awareness of the experimental group were compared, the critical ratio obtained was found to be significant at 0.01 level (CR = 42.79; p < 0.01).

7.3 SUMMARY OF THE FINDINGS

The study throws light on the fact that the prevailing health awareness level of women coir workers regarding occupational diseases are not satisfactory in all the select three dimensions. The study also found that the developed Multimedia Package on heath awareness regarding occupational diseases is effective in enhancing the awareness of women coir workers of coastal areas of Kerala.

7.4 REVIEW AND RECOMMENDATIONS

Coir retting industry is presently passing through difficult times, mainly due to the scarcity of raw materials, increased price of yarn and products and reduced inflow of orders from abroad. Coir Board in collaboration with the State Government may initiate proper steps for improving the status of this industry.

The premises of the retting yard situated in the Coastal areas of Kerala, are inhabited mainly by the community of people engaged in coir industry. Retting practices cause air and water pollution which adversely affects the community and ecosystem. In most coastal areas one of the major problems faced by the people engaged in retting activity is lack of safe drinking water. Also they need proper sanitation facilities.

Awareness programmes conducted in the various Wards of Anjengo Panchayath has raised their health awareness level regarding occupational as well as communicable diseases. Coir labourers receive very low wages from co-operative societies. It is most striking that worker especially women spent the whole day in the unhygienic conditions of the yard and finds hardly any time to spare for other educational and cultural activities. Low financial conditions compounded with illiteracy make their life miserable. Retting community deserves much support from the Government for the upliftment of their health as well as life status.

7.5 CONCLUSION

This project examined the health awareness level of coir retting women of coastal areas of Kerala, a state ranked at the top in terms of human development index, social development index and gender development index among the states in India. The state is often described as a land of 'good health at low cost' and is reported to have the lowest rural-urban inequalities in public health status. The present study highlights the need of additional awareness campaign for the women coir workers of coastal areas of Kerala which revealed the need of developing multimedia learning packages which can be used for training. The awareness campaign with the help of developed multimedia package proved very effective in empowering the coir retting women. The study also found that the multimedia Package on heath awareness regarding occupational diseases is effective in enhancing the awareness of women coir workers of coastal areas of Kerala.

BIBLIOGRAPHY

BIBLIOGRAPHY

Abdul Aziz, P.K., & Balakrishnan Nair, N. (1978). The nature of pollution in the retting zones of the backwaters of Kerala, *Aquatic Biology, 3*, 1978, pp. 41-62.

Abdul Aziz P.K., & Balakrishnan Nair, N. (1982). Ecology of Crustacean plankton of the retting zone with special reference to sulphide pollution in a backwater system of Kerala.
Mahasagar, 15 (3), 1982, pp. 175-183.

Abbassi S.A., Remani,K.N. (1982). Environmental pollution due to retting of coconut husk and preliminary studies on closed system retting. *Journal of Institution of Engineers*, 1982.

Antony A. & Nambissan, P.N.K. (1982). Variations of Polychaete in the polluted waters of Cochin areas. *Proceedings of National Seminar on "Mussel Watch"*.

Ajith Kumar B.S & Alagarswami,K. (1982). Effect of pollution due to coconut husk retting on reproductive potential of Green Mussel, Perna viridis. *Proceedings of National Seminar on "Mussel Watch"*.

Astleitner, H., & Keller, J. M. (1995). A model for motivationally adaptive computer-assisted instruction. **Journal of Research on Computing in Education, 27(3)**. Retrieved January 27, 2005, from Academic Search Premier.

Amitava, Mukherjee. (1995). *Participatory Rural Appraisal Methods and Applications in Rural Planning*, Vikas Publishing House, Ltd. New Delhi-110032, pp.433.

Balakrishnan Nair,N. (1983). Meiofauna of Edava Nadayara backwater system, South West Coast of India. *Mahasagar, 16*, pp. 55-65.

Balakrishnan Nair,N., & Abdul Aziz, (1984) Ecology of Indian Estuaries: Ecology and Distribution of Benthic Microfauna in the Ashtamudi Estuary of Kerala. *Mahasagar, 17*, pp.89-101.

Bhatt, J.V., Prabhu, G.N., Kundala, K.G., & Amuja, R. (1969). *'Investigations on Anaerobic Retting of Coconut Husk'*, 3rd International Congress on the 'Global Impacts of Applied Microbiology' Bombay, 39.

Captain R,Beavan. (1982). *Hand Book of Freshwater Fishes of India*, Narendra Publishing House, New Delhi, pp.247.

Damodaran, A.D., Pavithran, C., & Warrier. K.G.K. (1995). "Polycoir and Ught-Weight Bricks", *Souvenire—Seminar and Exhibition on Modernisation of Coir Industry*, pp.159.

Davis, C. Charles. (1955). *The Marine and Freshwater Plankton*. Michigan State University Press, pp. 562.

Fernandez, Christy. (2000). "Coir Industry in India", *CoirNews, August 20, 29(8)*, pp. 23-25.

Final report submitted to Kerala Research Programme on Local Level Development Centre for Development studies by *Centre for Water Resources Development and Management*, Kunnamangalam, Kozhikode, Kerala in April.

Flake, J. (1994). *Visioning About Technology and Learning*. Retrieved February 13, 2005, from http://mailer.fsu.edu/~jflake/AVISION.html

Gandhi,G.N. (2001). "Export of coir products in the emerging international business scenario", *Paper presented in the International Seminar on Coir at Kochi*, Oct. 11-13, pp.7.

Gabrielle, D. M. (2003). *The Effects of Technology-Mediated Instructional Strategies on Motivation, Performance and Self-Directed Learning*. Retrieved February 20, 2005, from http://etd.lib.fsu.edu/theses/available/etd-11142003—171019

Goel, Rameshwar. (2001). "Development of coir in domestic market", *Paper presented in the International Seminar on Coir at Kochi*, October 11-13.

House, J. D. (2003). The motivational effects of specific instructional strategies and computer use for mathematics learning in Japan: Findings from the third international mathematics and science study. *International Journal of Instructional Media, 30(1)*. Retrieved February 7, 2005, from Academic Search Premier.

Jhingran, V.G. (1982). *Fish and Fisheries of India*. Hindustan Publishing Corporation (India) Delhi, pp. 454.

Jayasankar N.P., & Menon, K.P.V. (1961). Microbiological Flora of A Few Coconut Retting Areas, *Coir (5)*, pp. 33-36.

Keller, J. M. (1979). Motivation and Instructional Design: A Theoretical Perspective. *Journal of Instructional Development, 2(4)*, pp.26-34.

Kutty, V.K. (1999). "Marketing strategy for promoting sales of coir products", *CoirNews, 28(1)*, pp. 21-23.

Lean, J., Mangles, T., & Moizer, J. (1999). Introducing computing and information systems. In Fallows, S. and Ahmet, K. (eds.) *Inspiring Students: Case Studies in Motivating The Learner*. (pp. 70-71), London: Kogan Page Limited.

Mathrubhumi Daily, 22nd September, 1999.

Mathrubhumi Daily, 14th May 2000.

Mathrubhumi Daily, 26th May 2000.

Malayala Manorama Daily, 18th May 2000.

Neela, Mukherjee. (1997). *Participatory Rural Appraisal—Methodology and Application*. Concept Publishing Company, New Delhi—110059, pp.160.

Remani, K.N. (1979). *Organic Pollution in Cochin Backwater with Special Reference to Benthos*. Ph.D Thesis, University of Cochin, 1979.

Remani, K.N., Venugopal,P., Sarala Devi,K., & Unnithan, R.V. (1980). *Retting As a Source of Pollution in Cochin Backwaters*. International Seminars, BARC, Bombay 1980.

Remani,K.N., Venugopal.P., Sarala Devi,K., & Unnithan R.V. (1981). Sediments of A Retting Yard. *Indian Journal of Marine Sciences*, 10 (1), pp. 41-44.

Remani K.N., Sarala Devi K., Venugopal, P., & Unnithan, R.V. (1983). Indicator Organisms of pollution in Cochin backwaters, *Mahasagar 16*, pp.199-207.

Remani, K.N., Nirmala,E., & Nair,S.R. (1989). Pollution Due To Coir Retting and Its Effect on Estuarine Flora and Fauna. *International Journal of Environmental Studies, Vol.32*, pp.285-295.

Remani K.N., & Nirmala,E. (1989). *Assessment of Pollution Due To Retting Of Coconut Husk and Development of Alternative Retting Technology*. Final Report, CWRDM.

Remani,K.N., Nirmala, E. & Nair,S.R. (1989). *Prediction and Assessment of the Biological Characteristics in the Retting Yards of Kerala*. National Seminar on "Aquatic Pollution and Strategies for Prevention and Management", December 18-20th 1989, Department of Aquatic Biology, University of Kerala.

Remani, K.N., Nirmala, E., Jalaja, T.K., Nirmala Stephen & Nair, S.R. (1990). "Status of Flora and Fauna in a Coir-retting Backwater Ecosystem". Seminar on *Water Quality Status of Kerala*, Cochin 1990, organised by CWRDM.

Sanacore, J. (1997). Promoting Lifetime Literacy through Authentic Self-Expression and Intrinsic Motivation. *Journal of Adolescent & Adult Literacy, 40(7)*, pp.568-71.

Sivaramakrishnan,R.(1999). New Generation Organic Fibre Coir Geomaterials for Environmental Solutions in the new Millennium, *Coir News, 28(12)*, Dec. 20, pp. 31-36.

The Hindu, Friday, August 4, 2000

Theroux, P. (1994). *Enhance learning with technology*. Retrieved February 13, 2005, from http://members.shaw.ca/priscillatheroux/motivation.html